As an associate director of the National Theatre during Peter Hall's tenure, Bill Bryden ran the Cottesloe Theatre, directing some of the greatest stage shows in popular memory, including the world premiere of Pulitzer Prize-winning *Glengarry Glen Ross*. Here, with characteristic candour, Bryden offers intimate sketches of his encounters – both on and off the stage – with some of the biggest stars of twentieth-century theatre, including Tennessee Williams, David Mamet, Helen Mirren, Arthur Miller, Laurence Olivier and Ralph Richardson. Bryden's words are matched by exclusive photographs from Nobby Clark; powerful portraits of the subjects in unguarded moments during rehearsal, and production shots that offer a striking visual record of these pioneering shows.

BRYDEN & CLARK

LIVES IN THE THEATRE

WORDS: BILL BRYDEN

PHOTOGRAPHS: NOBBY CLARK

First published in 2014 by Oberon Books Ltd

521 Caledonian Road, London N7 9RH

Tel: +44 (0) 20 7607 3637 / Fax: +44 (0) 20 7607 3629

e-mail: info@oberonbooks.com

www.oberonbooks.com

PB ISBN: 978-1-78319-083-6

E ISBN: 978-1-78319-582-4

Front cover: 'Six Characters in Search of an Author' BBC Studios Glasgow, 1992
Back cover: 'Willie Rough' contact sheet, Shaw Theatre, London, 1973
pii-iii: Mark McManus as Jesus Christ, 'The Passion', Easter Sunday, 1977

Printed and bound by Replika Press Pvt Ltd, India.

Visit www.oberonbooks.com to read more about all our books and to buy them. You will also find features, author interviews and news of any author events, and you can sign up for e-newsletters so that you're always first to hear about our new releases.

Contents

'The Big Picnic', Glasgow, The Shed, Govan, 1994

To Angela
'A lass unparalleled'

To: Kjelde & Helle

good names!

Much love Bill Bryson

This book could, certainly, be accused of 'name-dropping'. I plead guilty. I'm minded of my dear friend Michael Braun, who wrote *Love Me Do! – The Beatles' Progress* which – John Lennon claimed – was the best book about the band. Michael's conversation was always sprinkled with stars. He'd say 'Jack talked to Stanley about what to do about the movie and then he asked Roman who said to tell Francis to call Marlon and tell him it was a great part and say he would be working with Bernardo' – and so on and so forth. The English at dinner would upbraid New Yorker Braun: 'Michael would you stop name-dropping. Bernardo this, Kubrick that. It's not good manners.' Michael would reply: 'That's who they are!'

B.B.

Willie Rough

by Bill Bryden

Royal Lyceum Theatre, Edinburgh; Shaw Theatre, London

Cast of 'Willie Rough', Shaw Theatre, London, 1973

'There must be something big going on at the Usher Hall tonight,' said my mother to the Church of Scotland Minister, who had chartered a bus from Greenock to Edinburgh, when they both witnessed the lines around the block from the Hall to the Lyceum Theatre. The Minister replied 'The queue is for your son's play.'

My mother, unused to enthusiasm and most careful of praise, replied 'Oh.'

The play was *Willie Rough*, my first work as both a writer and director. It was an imaginative portrait of my maternal grandfather. He was a shipyard worker and what I would call a 'Christian socialist'. I placed him in the industrial conflict 'Red Clydesdale' in the First World War.

We lived in Greenock, where the Member of Parliament was Hector McNeil, the Secretary of State for Scotland with a huge majority. Nevertheless, other parties came knocking at Grandpa (Gagga's) door. 'Good evening. I am William Turpie, your Conservative candidate.' Willie Rough replies 'We vote Labour like everyone else but you can come in and have a dram…you're welcome.' The tired Conservative came in and had his glass of 'Springbank' from Campbeltown where as a family we went on holiday.

The important thing about *Willie Rough* was the company that performed it. The best actors in Scotland, all together as a genuine ensemble. A company, in my view, is like a football team – defence, midfield and attack. I remember at the time *The Scotsman* asked me who I thought was the best director in Britain. I had no hesitation in answering 'Alex Ferguson'. In the company, Roddy McMillan was 'capo de tutti capi'. He was a great actor, a fine writer and a moving singer. I learnt so much from his talent and I am still flattered that he gave me so much of his time and space and led me to believe that I had the makings of a director.

The whole company were stars – Fulton Mackay, John Cairney, James Grant, Joseph Brady et al. I mustn't forget the 'attack' – Paul Young and Andrew Byatt. Roddy led them as captain. All egos were sacrificed to the 'commonweal' of the team. The performances were accurate and wonderful. As Roddy said 'We're playing our fathers. There's no excuse.'

It was a wonderful time. My son Dillon was born. I took him to the revival of the play, years later with an inferior cast. I think he wondered what the remembered fuss had all been about. The acting then had been unmatched. My daughter Kate now has a son called Fulton after her godfather, Fulton Mackay. Lots of roads lead to *Willie Rough*. The reviews were unanimously good both in Edinburgh and London. The one 'carpee' was my local paper the *Greenock Telegraph*. The notice read: 'While *Willie Rough* is a good play, it is not a great play.' The words 'prophet', 'own' and 'country' come to mind.

P.S. While the play was in London I first met the photographer Nobby Clark. He made a series of stills in sepia. I still have them on the wall of my study.

4 Hayden Griffin & Zen, 2007
Opposite: Hayden Griffin (Designer) & Andy Phillps (Lighting Designer), National Theatre, 1983

O'Neill Season

The Long Voyage Home, The Iceman Cometh, Hughie

by Eugene O'Neill

National Theatre, Cottesloe

Hayden Griffin died only last year. One of the most distinguished stage designers of the British theatre, his work enhanced the plays of many of the most important writers of the contemporary stage, including Edward Bond, David Hare, Howard Brenton, David Mamet and John Osborne. But it is his work on the O'Neill season at the Cottesloe on which I've chosen to focus.

Our first O'Neill was the epic *The Iceman Cometh* at the Lyceum in Edinburgh. During his usual meticulous research, Hayden had found O'Neill's own pencil sketches he'd done while he was writing the play – his memory of the pub on Fulton Street in New York, this side of the Brooklyn Bridge. Hayden's enhancement

of this 'placement' by the author provided a set that has never been improved for that great play.

The Edinburgh production, starring the explosive Ian Bannen as Hickey, was a success but, if the chance came, I decided a season of O'Neill's plays, early and late, would be a fitting tribute to the writer who was, after all, the architect of the American theatre.

John Ford had always been my director hero. You have only to be among the chaos of a Hollywood set for a Western, with its wranglers, armourers, best boys and the rest, to realise that Ford was a genius in making something personal and poetic out of this circus. Of all of Ford's great films, one of my favourites has always been *The Long Voyage Home*, based on O'Neill's early one-act 'sea' plays, photographed in deep focus by the unique Greg Toland. These early plays would be the start of the season to include, of course *Iceman* and the late virtual monologue which is *Hughie*, for which Stacy Keach agreed to come over from New York to play at the National. The action takes place in the old Royalton Hotel, where O'Neill stayed when in the city. There is an elevator in the lobby. It went nowhere in the Cottesloe but due to Hayden's sleight of hand and the lighting of Andy Phillips, I for one, believed it went through all floors to the penthouse.

We achieved the O'Neill season through the encouragement of Peter Hall, the production management of Jason Barnes, the commitment of the company and most of all by Hayden's design and the lighting of Andy Phillips. I'm not forgetting the wonderful work Hayden did for other directors – the whirlwind scheme for David Hare's *Plenty* and the marvellous *Pravda*, or his work for Bill Gaskill at the Court and beyond.

Both Hayden and I, in a comforting embrace, watched Andy Phillips's life end. I did not volunteer to witness Hayden's demise. Nobby held vigil. I prefer to remember the argumentative, brilliant, meticulous, brave artist whose designs blazed across our stages.

| Stacy Keach as Hughie, 1980

(above) Ann Lynn, Jack Shepherd, Morag Hood, Edna Doré in The 'Iceman Cometh', 1980;
(below) 'The Long Voyage Home', 1979

from an occasional diary

My stage manager was dating an actor. She decided to take him home to meet her parents. At the time the actor was playing the role of a fascist skinhead – swastikas tattooed on his bald head, attitude, and a pronounced cockney accent. The visit was not a success. Months later, she decided to take the actor to meet her parents for a second time. On this visit he was playing the role of a long-haired bohemian. A cut glass accent, a slight lisp and wearing a smart velvet jacket. When the actor had left, my stage manager friend asked her father 'Well Dad, what do you think?' 'Oh, much better, darling. Much more suitable than that other actor fella you brought home last time. Much better!'

The actor was one and the same. His name – Daniel Day-Lewis.

Daniel Day-Lewis as Kafka in 'The Insurance Man' by Alan Bennett, 1986

The Royal Court

One of my great regrets is that I never met George Devine. In the theatre, memory is short, so there may be many who have never heard of him or his achievements. George Devine was the energy behind the English Stage Company at the Royal Court Theatre in Sloane Square, Chelsea, London. It had been a variety venue as well as a playhouse of Shaw and Granville Barker. It was declared 'a writer's theatre' with the unique mission of a 'right to fail' by Devine and his associates, the most important of whom was Tony Richardson. It was they who championed John Osborne's *Look Back in Anger* in 1956 and, as they say, the rest is history. It certainly was. Years later when Ken Tynan was dramaturg of Olivier's National he tried to commission Osborne: 'John, come with Larry and me and make history.' Osborne's reply: 'I've made history'.

Osborne's love and gratitude to Devine is evident in his heartfelt obituary to his friend in *The Observer*, copied verbatim in his classic biography *A Better Class of Person*. Bill Gaskill, Devine's successor as director at the Royal Court, more than kept his spirit alive and fanned the flame of his burning light. My contemporaries there, including Christopher Hampton, David Hare and Nicholas Wright, would all, I'm sure, vouch to that.

Gaskill encouraged us all. It was a unique apprenticeship – not always flattering but never patronising. He developed and took chances on distinctive actors like Jack Shepherd, Dennis Waterman and in particular, Victor Henry. More than that, he championed the writing of the unique Edward Bond.

Bill Gaskill is a great director – a master of the stage. We learned a little from him, but I'm afraid he didn't tell us it all. So, Gaskill kept George Devine's work alive and his memory potent.

When Devine died there was a glorious tribute to his life at the Old Vic. This included extracts from all the Royal Court plays over which he had presided, climaxing with a piece from *The Entertainer* by John Osborne starring Laurence Olivier. One of Sir Laurence's other duties of the evening was supervising a scene from *The Kitchen* by Arnold Wesker, based on the legendary production by John Dexter, at the Court.

The all-star cast on this great occasion included Vanessa Redgrave, Robert Stephens and, would you believe, Noël Coward portraying a Maltese chef. After running the scene and 'The Master' giving his best Maltese, Larry interrupted: 'Noëly baby, what accent is that you are using?' Coward replied: 'Stage foreign.'

10 | 'The World Turned Upside Down' by Keith Dewhurst, National Theatre 1978, Bill Bryden, Sebastian Graham-Jones & Keith Dewhurst
Opposite: 'The World Turned Upside Down' by Keith Dewhurst, National Theatre 1978

John Grierson

John Grierson was the first great man I ever met. He dubbed the documentary film 'the creative treatment of actuality'. What his view would be of the present rash of *Big Brother* and the like does not bear thinking about. Not many remember John Grierson, so let me remind the young of his stature and describe his influence on me.

His first claim to fame was directing *Drifters*, about the harrowing lives of Scottish fishermen before the war. It was to become his finest hour as he headed the G.P.O. Film Unit – the country's leading propaganda machine – with a crowd of celebrated associates including Granada's Dennis Foreman, the writer John Mortimer, the poet W.H. Auden and the composer Benjamin Britten.

'Night Mail', about the journey of the mail train from London to Scotland, is the highlight of that work, with Auden's verse set to the rhythm of rails:

> 'This is the night mail
> Crossing the Border
> Bringing the cheque
> And the Postal Order'.

'Clackety clack' go the rails and the verse with Britten's marvellous music as counterpoint. Grierson was often accused of not giving credit to his collaborators, taking ownership and plaudits to himself. He could hardly diminish the work of Auden and Britten, but he was often blamed for lessening the contribution of 'Night Mail's' director, Harry Watt.

Canada has seldom been a centre of world cinema. This led to the Hollywood joke: 'How do you guarantee a flop? Shoot it in Canada and have Donald Sutherland play the lead.' Sadly, many such projects went 'straight to Blockbusters'. However, years before, there was a wonderful idea from the government of the Dominion. This was the formation of the National Film Board of Canada and the inspired idea to invite John Grierson to be its leader and its conscience. At the Film Board, Grierson encouraged many near-perfect documentary films – *Corral and Manolete* in particular was a unique movie made up of still images of the great matador. He encouraged the unique, Scots-born animator Norman McLaren at this time. He also met the newspaper tycoon Roy Thomson, who eventually was awarded the Scottish franchise for the newly formed ITV. Thomson described this as 'a licence to print money', as few would forget. Part of Thomson's licence submission for the franchise was a programme overseen and run by Grierson called *This Wonderful World*. During the course of this, the only network programme Scottish TV had on the ITV network, I met and worked with the great Grierson and my standards in work were, I suppose, found. I hope his influence has never left me and his tenets still prevail.

My elevation from junior researcher to working with Grierson was caused by the illness of his regular assistant and I was more than flattered to fill the breach. I presented myself to the great man's office and awaited instructions. 'Bryden,' (never Christian names) 'They have a high regard for your future around these parts, so there are some jobs which I'm entrusting to you. First, you have to go to the Accounts Department and collect this week's expenses float and then at two thirty bring the cash and settle the lunch bill at Ferrari.' Grierson held court at Ferrari, a Glasgow Italian restaurant, famous before Alvaro and the others conquered the King's Road in London.

Grierson's regular table for six was always full of acolytes. Some disciples, many hangers-on and the flotsam and jetsam of no-hopers, and has-beens and never-would-bes. Grierson never minded the obvious lack of talent around him. He was wisdom, the oracle. He was Grierson. Flattery kept him going as he kept 'the table on a roar'. I came with the float to settle the bill. Sometimes I was allowed a whisky to hear the end of the discourse. Even when John was in fine form – witty, erudite, full of artistic sense – his guests were not gifted enough to benefit. In the Accounts Department I announced I was there to collect Dr Grierson's expenses for the week. 'Would £500 be enough?' asked the clerk. £500? In 1963! I nodded in the affirmative, collected the large

white fivers and prepared to pay for lunch for Grierson and his guests. Often, when filling in the expense form, he made sure the weekly tally would total, say, £498 and twelve shillings no matter what the truth of it might be.

The above was just about the extent of my job, until one day I think I impressed him. He came bounding into the office: 'Bryden – get me Jack Warner on the phone immediately!' When I suggested that the time in Los Angeles was three thirty in the morning and the famous Warner Brother might be asleep. All Grierson said was: 'Good thinking.' After that moment I think I was trusted.

This Wonderful World was a programme of documentary extracts, edited by Grierson, of films directed by his 'friends'. 'My friend, Arne Sucksedorf' made films about woodpeckers. 'My friend Hilary Harris', who directed the seminal Clyde shipbuilding film *Seawards the Great Ships* (for which, as the producer, Grierson took for himself much of the credit) did a highly original piece called *Subway*. All 'my friends' sent their film to Grierson for his approval and inclusion in the show.

In editing, he never used a Moviola or a Steenbeck bench, but a piece of white card. The film would be projected onto a sheet. He raised the white card across the projector beam for the beginning of the cut and again for its end. Nothing changed the cutting from the white card decisions – from white sheet to the finished programme. He sensed the rhythm of film like no other.

His advice on unfinished movies was valued not only by 'my friends', but makers of film the world over.

One of the films he championed was Bert Stern's movie on the Newport Festival, *Jazz on a Summer's Day*: a fabulous picture. It was the first show I did with him, and pleasingly it got wider distribution than normally granted for a documentary film.

We ended the programme with the great Mahalia Jackson singing The Lord's Prayer. At its end, after a pause, Grierson, the great communicator said: 'Mahalia Jackson – a woman whom God has tapped upon the shoulder. I wish you in the Highlands and the Lowlands, over the border and over the sea, a very good night.'

Was it the memory of the prayer or his close that had the hard-nosed crew wiping away a tear as the credits rolled? A bit of both, I suspect. I'll never forget that we applauded to a man as soon as we were off the air. 'Bryden, get everybody a dram!' The entire crew was taken to The Top Spot, the pub next to the studio for drinks and I remember I had the float. Drinks taken, Grierson pulled me aside. 'Bryden – you could be quite good. What are you doing in this abattoir of talent?'

So, farewell the £500 float and farewell Scotland (for a while). Go South, young man! I will never forget his hard care and his example. When I watch these so-called documentaries and actuality shows of today I remember Grierson's definition of the documentary as 'the creative treatment of actuality'. Where is the creativity in the hidden camera? The people behind such lazy work are not the inheritors of Grierson's dictum but a blight on his legacy.

Years later I was directing my first National Theatre production at the Old Vic: *Spring Awakening*, in a wonderful version by Edward Bond. Among the cast were Peter Firth and the late, and much lamented, Cyril Cusack. Now Peter was the talk of the town in Peter Shaffer's play *Equus*. Famous people came into his dressing room to congratulate him after every performance. At tea break the rest of us wanted to know who had been 'round' the previous week. 'Richard Burton and Elizabeth Taylor, Henry Kissinger and Nancy, Neil Kinnock, the Prince of Wales' – the guest list went on. After a pause, sipping his tea, Cyril Cusack volunteered: 'I knew W.B. Yeats'. Well, I knew John Grierson.

from an occasional diary

So, Colin Welland has won the Oscar for Best Screenplay for *Chariots of Fire*. Good. He made a speech: 'The British are coming.' Bad. Very bad. In the first place no one in the audience knew it was a parody of Paul Revere. It was taken as a threat to every American screenwriter. It must have cost the British contingent in L.A. many a dollar. 'Bill, are you one of these people who've come over the pond to take all of our jobs?' That was Billy Wilder, to whom I'd been introduced on my first visit to L.A..

Wilder, the nonpareil of writer/directors had taken everyone British as a threat. Contracts were cancelled. 'Go' projects became development deals and, I suppose, rather than 'coming' the British went home. Colin had his comeuppance at the Baftas when he lost to Bill Forsyth's *Local Hero*. As an actor, Colin should have been aware that, as a nominee, the camera is on you so you keep smiling and clapping even if you are not the winner. No such luck. A face like thunder and disappointment akin to bereavement. 'His gas is in a peep, now,' said my Scottish friend, not hiding his glee at his friend Forsyth's triumph.

Welland's folly was not the only fallout from *Chariots*. Its producer David Puttnam, was made, briefly, Head of Production at Columbia Pictures. The worst kind of new broom, he had the Hollywood people gloating at his failure at the job. 'He refused to kiss Bill Cosby's ass.' 'He turned down projects from the producer, Ray Stark, and he was on the Board!' Both of these decisions might be laudable but on the Coast they seemed less like naivety, more like insanity.

When I read recently in the Property Section of a newspaper 'Oscar Winner's House for Sale', how did I know it was the Welland pile?

When the best of British films were made for BBC Television Welland did good work. His best achievement, in my opinion, was discovering and encouraging the Scots dramatist and Prix Italia winner, Peter McDougall, whose unique voice burned the airwaves from that day to this.

Veronica Quilligan as Wendla Bergmann and Peter Firth as Melchior Gabor
in 'Spring Awakening' by Frank Wedekind, Old Vic, National Theatre, 1974

Jane Carr as Martha Bessel and Jenny Agutter as Thea
in 'Spring Awakening' by Frank Wedekind, Old Vic, National Theatre, 1974

Opera

Billy Connolly has a routine of a dying friend being interviewed.

The questioner says, 'There's the good news and the bad news.'

The patient asks, 'What's the bad news?'

'You have three days to live.'

'And the good news?' asks the dying patient.

'The fellow in the next bed might want to buy your slippers!'

Entering the world of opera was a similar dilemma. The good news was that I was encouraged to direct by three brilliantly talented conductors – Bernard Haitink, Leonard Bernstein and Simon Rattle. The bad news was the first project was to be Richard Wagner's *Parsifal*.

Parsifal

by Richard Wagner
Conducted by Bernard Haitink

Royal Opera House, Covent Garden

My move from the new National Theatre to the Royal Opera House, I presumed, would be a sea change, not that my little boat would be forever in angry seas heading for the rocks. In my first days, I realised why Peter Hall had resigned there as Director of Productions.

The 'admin' love the stories of the Tosca you've rehearsed for a month being indisposed and another

Bernard Haitink in rehearsal, 1988

voice, who is, at the moment, in Buenos Aires, and has not rehearsed the production, is willing to fly in (if the money is right) and wear whatever dress fits and the show must go on!

The admin refer to the building as a 'house'. I begged to differ, telling them: 'I *live* in a house – I *work* in a theatre.' This fell on deaf ears. I'm sure they hoped that Haitink would fire me. As to the opera, it is in German, so my folly, I suppose, was not to improve my knowledge. My A-level was based on 'Das Buch der Jugend', in which young Germans went camping and yodelling and their adventures, more often than not, ended with 'Wir lachen laut!'

I admit my preparation in Wagner's language was sparse, but I was completely taken aback by the 'religion': the singers, mostly German, worshipped Wagner.

Unanswered prayers were made to his shrine in Bayreuth, where every major director, apart from the great exception, Patrice Chéreau, perished. I found this obeisance to a composer of questionable politics obscene. I will not continue, but suffice to say, I made a friend of the great bass, Robert Lloyd, who believed in what I was trying to do. I have to say that Bernard conducted all the colours of the score brilliantly.

In retrospect, the only good news about *Parsifal* was, during the course of rehearsal, I met Angela Douglas and we lived happily ever after. Out of the shipwreck, the boat sailed on.

20 Peter Seiffert as Parsifal, Waltraud Meier as Kundry, 1988
Opposite: John Dobson as a Knight of the Grail, with the Swan, 1988

from an occasional diary

The Baron was a television series sponsored by Lew Grade. In the days when any American, or even Canadian actor was, in the eyes of the money men, better than British, the title role was played by Steve Forrest. Steve's claim to fame was that he was the brother of the film star, Dana Andrews.

Now, Steve was a drinker, a gambler and not much of a sleeper. He would come onto the studio set in early morning looking worse for wear and twenty years too old to play the role.

A shower, a wig and make-up would transform Steve into 'The Baron'. He looked younger, more orange, and embalmed.

In one particular episode, stuntmen were involved. When Forrest emerged from his transformation from the old reprobate to juvenile, one stuntman, by the name of Alf Joint, shouted at him 'Keep moving, Steve. Keep moving! They're doing a stock-check at Madame Tussauds.'

The Cunning Little Vixen

By Leoš Janáček, conducted by Simon Rattle

Royal Opera House, Covent Garden

Returning to the Royal Opera House for *Vixen* was like travelling to a different country. It was as if someone had lifted the roof from the building to let the sunshine in. The difference was, in a word, *enthusiasm*. Simon Rattle had helped translate the work from Serbo-Croat to English so, believe it or not, it was billed as the first foreign opera to be 'sung in English' at the Garden. And what a cast of glorious singers Simon had assembled. Thomas Allen, Robert Tear, Gwynne Howell and, in the title role, the delightful Lillian Watson.

Part of my luck was that I had persuaded Stuart Hopps, master of form and dance who knew the work, to collaborate with me on the project. His contribution to its success and to its many revivals is incalculable. His loyalty I will always treasure. Another, and important, reason for this new atmosphere was that Jeremy Isaacs had been appointed General Director. Jeremy had come from television and, while his deep knowledge of opera was sometimes questioned, his love of it – never.

Simon Rattle in rehearsal, 1980

Jeremy had longed to be Director-General of the BBC. I am of the opinion that he and Brian Wenham were the two best D.G.s the BBC never had. Jeremy told me of his interview. The first comment from one of the governors on the panel was not even a question but a criticism: 'Mr Isaacs, you look like a man who doesn't like taking orders.' The BBC's loss was the Garden's gain.

Part of the enthusiasm was the brilliant casting director, Peter Katona, looking further for young voices he was sure would grace the spotlight.

Even the 'crush bar' – often a solemn silence at the interval – was energised by Alan, the droopy-moustached barman…with his engaging personality. As Harold Pinter said to me at the premiere of *Vixen*: 'It's new, I mean – it's a brand-new situation'. The joy of the new! Bill Dudley made a unique design for the opera and, thank God that my team and Simon's with the orchestra and the singers made more than a creative marriage. These perfect times are rare. On the first night, the difficult work of the aerial artists, Deborah Pope as the spirit of the Vixen

24 | 'Cunning Little Vixen' in rehearsal, 1980.
| Robert Tear (with sticks) and Frog

sink – everything to ensure her privacy. Meanwhile, in the kitchen – Arthur with his Mother:

Miller: 'Well, Mom, what d'ya think?'

Mother: 'Well, Artie, she's as you said, really beautiful, good manners, funny…'

Arthur waited for his mother's 'but', and it soon came.

Mother: 'But she pisses like a horse!'

Eventually, we at last discussed the project at hand: *The Crucible*. Miller had seen a school production near his home in Connecticut and was bowled over by the girls playing the witches, especially in Act Three where they 'see' the bird on the ceiling of the Courthouse. 'It was truly hysterical. Truly sexy – never worked like that before. It was puberty I guess. That's my note. Look for it'. We agreed that we were in search of 'jailbait' for the Salem children. Found. With superb Caroline Embling, the serene Valerie Whittington and 'real bait', the sixteen-year-old Gina Bellman. Paraphrasing Miss Jean Brodie, I heard myself addressing the male members of my cast.

'This is Gina, she is my favourite and any involvement with her during the run will result in a one-way ticket from Waterloo to Wandsworth!' It was a fortunate decision to do a 'good play'. We happily transferred to The Comedy Theatre in the West End. Hayden Griffin did a marvellous Puritan set and all my players were on top form – especially my girls. I can remember the chilling effect of their energy when confronted by 'the bird' on the ceiling of the court. They raised the roof.

The Silver Tassie

by Mark Anthony Turnage,

After Sean O'Casey

English National Opera — Coliseum

Bill Bryden on the gun for 'The Silver Tassie' Opera, ENO, 2000

I question him about actors – 'Well, Marlon was always the best. Everybody knows that. Even Larry, but he won't admit it. You know who was the best for me? Eli Wallach. He was fixed to do Maggio in Zinnemann's *From Here to Eternity* and he had promised Kazan and me he'd play Kilroy in *Camino Real* (he always pronounced it 'Camino Reel'); He kept his promise. Maybe he's not the very best but he is my favourite.' Tennessee urged me to do *Small Craft Warnings*. 'It's your play, Bill.'

Finally we did the play at the Arcola Theatre in Dalston to some success. The cast included Jack Shepherd, a long-term and cherished colleague, Sian Thomas and Greg Hicks, who were wonderful, and the excellent Meredith MacNeill from Canada – 'Buzz' – called so because the great actor, Burgess Meredith was always called Buzz.

A week after our meeting, Tennessee Williams died at the unfashionable but funky Elysee Hotel in New York City. He had choked on a cap trying to open a bottle of pills.

He is immortal.

In his infant notebooks, T.W. said something I've never forgotten. There is a childlike drawing of a rainbow. Above it, this text:

'I have just found the beginning of The Rainbow. And I hope it so interesting that you won't want me to find an end.'

from an occasional diary

'A Western a contender for the Palme d'Or? I don't think so!'

The Western was then, as now, as dead as the rumba. It can be argued that Clint Eastwood gave it some later status when his *Unforgiven* won a clutch of Academy Awards. In those days however, a Western was too common to win. As for me, I was delighted and flattered that *The Long Riders*, my screenplay about the Jesse James-Younger gang, was one of the American entries to Cannes. Why couldn't a Western win?

I knew nothing about the festival until Lindsay Anderson won in 1969. At that time I was assistant to Bill Gaskill at the Royal Court, and in charge of bouquets for each and every triumph for one of the short list of people who were judged part of the Royal Court 'family.' In the bar next to the Court Tony Richardson told me; 'Billy, there's Lindsay, leather jacket and flat cap, dressed up as Brecht and *starving* on his private income and now *If...* his boys-at-public-school fantasy wins at Cannes. I think he deserves a bouquet! Call Connie [Constance Spry, the Mayfair florist] – he'll be in a suite at the Carlton now he's won, maybe he's stayed in "digs" – but I doubt it.'

The flowers were sent. The Cannes festival, as I found, was all about selling. Agents, bookers and 'phonies' are selling films that have been made and posters for movies that would be made or never made. In one of my years I saw one of these posters which boldly proclaimed 'Dustin Hoffman in *LaBrava*!' Below this headline in very small print (spectacles required) – 'Subject to Contract!' The film was never made.

It is a nightmare of negotiation to no point. The only 'deal' I've ever seen made was by my dear lost friend Philip Jones, who managed to 'sell' every territory in an hour for Robert Altman's *Vincent & Theo*, about Van Gogh and his brother. Philip was such that when countries tried to 'pass', he left until they *begged* to come back for more. Philip was a salesman – also a cherished friend – and made more money for many people than he made for himself. I've digressed since the thrill of my Western at Cannes. The second American entry that year was *All That Jazz*, a first-class film by the director and choreographer Bob Fosse. Fosse was a fabulous guy and fellow smoker (more than me – more than anybody).

The film deserves a re-visit. Wonderfully photographed by Fellini's Giuseppe Rotunno and, I'm sure, knowing Fosse, a struggle – whose life is in his work.

One day at the Carlton Hotel, where nominees stay, I noticed Fosse 'came on' to every young girl he saw. It is a common and insane thought that all choreographers are gay. Fosse played that cliché to the full. He would go up to a young girl, change her hairstyle with a touch, and discuss the length of her hem and the colour of her shoes and intimate details I could never know. Over dinner (or drinks, as Bob wouldn't eat) the nominees would meet. One of us decided to ask Bob Fosse the question. 'Bobby, you look gay but you seem to me to be pretty adroit at "romance" but I have a question.'

'What's that?' said Bob.

'They all seem so young – the girls. Why?'

Bob replied 'Their life stories are shorter!'

Bill Bryden, 1988

from an occasional diary

Al Pacino has been a pal to both Angela and me for a good while. We have had many lunches and dinners, talking at length on the art of acting. The following is one of the memorable encounters:

New York City.

Scene. Al Pacino's apartment. Christmas Eve family gathering. It went something like this...

Al: 'Angela...you love it here in the city?'

Angela: 'Oh, yes.'

Al: 'Is there anyone you'd like to meet?'

Angela: 'I'd love to meet Robert De Niro!'

Al: 'Oh. Won't I do?'

Al Pacino as Teach in 'American Buffalo', 1978

Dispatches

by Michael Herr

National Theatre, Cottesloe

Michael Herr & Tim Page in rehearsal for 'Dispatches', National Theatre 1979

'Thousands of people died in Vietnam that night, the twelve across the field, a hundred more along the road between the camp and the Can Tho hospital compound where I worked all the next day, not a reporter or a shooter but a medic, unskilled and scared. When we got back to camp that night I threw away the fatigues I'd been wearing. And for the next six years I saw them all, the ones I had really seen and the ones I'd imagined, theirs and ours, friends I'd loved and strangers, motionless figures in a dance, the old dance. Years of thinking this or that about what happens to you when you pursue a fantasy until it becomes experience, and then afterwards you can't handle the experience. Until I felt that I was a dancer too.'**

Just a short extract from *Dispatches* – Michael Herr's definitive journal of the 'rock and roll' war in Vietnam. A moment only, introducing the richness and scatological originality of his unique language. This was a book, a subject, and an author with whom I was determined to engage. In this backward glance, of all the projects we made as an ensemble called the Cottesloe Company, *Dispatches* was the best work.

I first became aware of the book when I watched a television discussion. The guest was the novelist John Le Carré, who enthusiastically proclaimed – 'This is the best book I have ever read on men and war in our time.' I was flabbergasted by Herr's wit, courage, and originality. The idea was to use the Cottesloe company in a Platform performance before the main evening show to help sales of the book. By the time I got round to this, *Dispatches* was a bestseller worldwide. So – no help wanted. It had to be a full-blown show if we could ever capture the essence of the book and the nature of the 'rock and roll war' and Michael's unique point of view. Peter Hall read the book on a Sunday and, as I remember, in a lift urged me to 'go for it'.

First things first, I had to meet Michael Herr and find out his views on an adaptation for our Theatre. We met in a busy burger bar in Sheridan Square in Greenwich Village in New York. Directors spend their time studying behaviour and there were two things I remember about that first meeting. First of all, he tore the filter tips from his French cigarettes and inserted what seemed to be birdseed into the remains. He took a long, deep drag and seemed 'better'. It was not birdseed. More remarkably, he had what Leonard Bernstein called 'the third ear' (i.e. what you've heard, what you're hearing, and 'third' telling the orchestra what you *want* to hear).

Michael could be totally engrossed in our conversation but hear others in the crowded steakhouse. 'Absolutely,' he would say to the tables nearby 'you bet!' and 'Don't do it. Don't ya do it.' while totally

Michael Feast as Mayhew, 1979

'Dispatches' at the National

THESE 'Vietnam' photographs were taken during rehearsal of the National Theatre's new production 'Dispatches' which opens on Wednesday.

The play is an adaptation of Michael Herr's book based on what he saw and heard during his three years covering the Vietnam war.

It tells how the 'grunts' lived their war. Dope, rock and roll, and trying not to get killed.

The photographs are by Nobby Clark who also chose the quotes from the book.

' Come on,' the Captain said, ' we'll take you out to play cowboys and Indians.'

When the 173rd held services for their dead from Dak To, the boots of the dead were arranged in formation on the ground.

' Boo-sheeit ! I ain't never gettin ' hit in Vietnam.' Michael Feast as Mayhew.

' Sure was some nice mornin'. Oh, man they can' jus' leave us alone one time ? ' Oscar James as Daytripper.

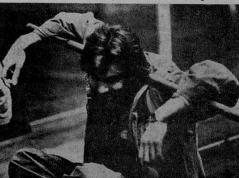

' There's gone be a death in my family. Just soon's I git home.' And then he laughed. Oliver Cotton as Orrin.

' General, what about the defence at Khe Sanh ? ' James Grant as Peter Braestrup.

Jack Shepherd as The Correspondent.

Don Warrington as Swinging Dick

The Helicopter in 'Dispatches' by Michael Herr, National Theatre, 1979, during performance

engaged in the embryo of my plan to turn the book of his recent life into a show.

Subsequent meetings in New York went well and, luckily, Michael's plan was to move his wife and family to London so he would be here for consultation on the script and, especially important, for rehearsals.

I decided to take on the adaptation myself, with Trevor Ray as my script editor. He was ruthless but always encouraging, and finally, we had a draft good enough from which to cast. Bill Dudley, as usual, designed a brilliant environment for the show, including the landing of a helicopter. I always thought that the heralded 'coup de theatre' in the musical *Miss Saigon* was déjà vu to the Cottesloe audience.

Jack Shepherd played Herr, or as we called him 'The Correspondent', Michael Feast, Derek Newark and James Grant were among the 'regulars' but the joy was to work with a wonderful group of black actors including Don Warrington, Oscar James and the fabulous Clarke Peters who had come to live in London from the US and taught many of the cast the rhythm of the piece. I was not at all surprised when he later found fame in *The Wire*.

A mention too, of Derek Thompson, a deeply gifted Belfast-born player who later found a role in *Casualty*.

He has been in the show for years and has made more than a good living for himself and his family but I wish he had spent more time in the theatre and in films. He was very fine in *Dispatches* but it is not a director's job to tell actors, no matter how talented, how to deal with their career.

During the technical rehearsals in Bill's wonderful space, lit by Andy Phillips, the real people from the book turned up, including the photographer Tim Page, and the author himself. When the action was at its height and, hopefully, at its most realistic, Page would drop down from the 'bleachers' and take a shot or two.

Finally (and I could go on with my memory of this production) John Tams considered there would be no live music to compete with the recorded rock classics referred to in the book and the script. Thank God he was persuaded otherwise, since his work and that of his band, The Home Service, was triumphant.

This was, indeed, the best. Perhaps the beginning of the end, but, as Trevor Ray said to me, as we were beginning to get it right:

'These are the good old days.'

Bill Bryden in rehearsal for 'Dispatches', 1979

The Irish Plays

The Playboy of the Western World

by J.M. Synge. National Theatre, Old Vic, Lyttelton and Olivier

The Plough and the Stars

by Sean O'Casey. National Theatre, Olivier

'I want this to be the definitive *Playboy*,' said I to the actor.

'*I* was the definitive Playboy' the actor replied.

I was dining with Cyril Cusack at the Randolph Hotel in Oxford after a performance on the tour of *Spring Awakening*, my first production for the National. He was wonderful in that play but still declined the role of the landlord, Michael James, in the great Irish play.

Often underestimated is the contribution of Irish writing to the canon of great drama. Where would writing for the theatre be without Sheridan, Congrave, Goldsmith, Wilde, O'Casey, Beckett, Synge, Brendan Behan, Brian Friel – and the young, like Martin McDonagh and Billy Roche.

Playboy, even without Cusack, had a great Irish cast. Around the theatre, the company was nicknamed 'the Abbey National.' The one exception was Susan Fleetwood. An English rose amongst the thorns of Ireland. She was magnificent.

Stephen Rea was the Playboy and wonderful he was. For a play that was scheduled for eighteen performances at the Old Vic but ran for eighteen months, Stephen was integral to its longevity. As was Jim Norton as Sean. I long to do *Waiting for Godot* with Stephen and Jim but they are often on different continents. If they are ever in Timbuktu at the same time I would be happy to direct it with them there.

We had great music from Paddy Moloney and The Chieftains, a great set from Geoffrey Scott who I had

worked with in Edinburgh and, all in all, *Playboy* was one of the happiest times of my professional life. Cyril Cusack joined us to play Fluther Good in *The Plough and the Stars* and, born to play the role, his performance was matchless. In rehearsal he became O'Casey's representative on earth. His comments were invaluable. Commenting on the scene between Susan and Tony Doyle he said, moved, 'This is the best love scene there has ever been' and he was thrilled when the soldiers in the coda actually had the London voices of Gawn Grainger and Glyn Grain. Again the set was by Geoffrey Scott. The music was by the great Armagh singer and banjo player Tommy Makem of The Clancy Brothers. Bernard Levin, then critic of *The Sunday Times*, headlined his review 'Two Cheers for O'Casey.' I, biased though I am, would have given four.

I leave the last word to Cusack. Robert De Niro had come over with friends, John Cassavetes and Harvey Keitel, to see *Glengarry Glen Ross* by David Mamet. My team all fell in love and in deep admiration of De Niro. It was 'Bobby' this and 'Bobby' that and 'Bobby' all the time. When we learned that Cusack was about to do the film *True Confessions* with De Niro and Robert Duvall, all my colleagues were interested in was how Cyril would deal with the great De Niro. Cyril, as usual, had a word for it.

'The thing is – in the film Robert is a priest – but I am a Cardinal. '

Cyril Cusack, Old Vic Theatre, 1980

54

A Month in the Country

by Ivan Turgenev, translated by Richard Freeborn. Albery Theatre, London

I have always been a company man. I believe an ensemble, at its best, can have the magic a great star performance has. However, some plays demand the individual talent of the unique artist.

I had seen Turgenev's *A Month in the Country* at both the National and by the Royal Shakespeare Company without the essential star performance, so I was not sure about the producer Duncan Weldon's invitation to direct the play in London's West End. The play was based on Turgenev's unrequited love of a great Russian opera star. A diva.

We were so fortunate that a real diva wished to perform the role. Helen Mirren was perfect in the part.

She was supported by a fabulous cast of talented friends – John Hurt, Polly Adams, John Standing, Trevor Ray and Gawn Grainger. Also, we lucked in to have Joseph Fiennes and the Irish actress, Anna Livia Ryan, as the young lovers.

Again a brilliantly accurate set by Hayden Griffin. Wonderfully lit by Andy Phillips with, as usual, perfect period costumes by Deirdre Clancy.

Everything resulted in a master West End hit but the triumph was Helen's.

Since that time, she has been made a Dame, played the Queen (twice) and been awarded an Oscar. She is deeply gifted and <u>funny</u>.

Helen is a wonderful comedienne (or is it 'comedian' nowadays). I would love her not to leave the comic parts to her fellow dames – Maggie and Judi.

It was a marvellous and special time working with Helen Mirren. Here's to the next!

It is impossible to leave this page without telling my second favourite Noël Coward story. Coward was in New York doing cabaret at the famous Carlyle Hotel when an aficionado was determined that he attend a matinee of a production at Lincoln Center. The play was *Three Sisters* by Chekhov. Uncut. Three and more hours of it. And set in the American Civil War, Vershinin and his garrison dressed in Southern Confederate uniforms. So what did the Master make of this? 'A month in the wrong country!' his reply when asked his opinion.

Helen Mirren as Natalya Petrovna & John Hurt as Ratkitin, 1994

Sir Peter Hall meeting The Queen & Sir Laurence Olivier
National Theatre, Royal Opening, 1976

To be fair, the chairman, Lord Rayne's, ambition, at the end of all this, was for the National to be dubbed 'Royal'.

Without Max Rayne the National would never have been completed. His expertise in property caused builders, clerks of works and all other construction departments to quake in their shoes. I saw this first-hand. Max and his wife Jane were very helpful to me in the Cottesloe days.

'Maybe Max could do something.'

I think this comment was by Michael Blakemore because nobody laughed.

'What can I do?' said Harry Birtwistle.

'You could do a new version of 'God Save The Queen' said the always enthusiastic Kustow. 'Not me – but I know somebody who can.' One by one the associates wriggled out of the event.

'I'm in Hollywood – sorry,' said Schlesinger.

Pinter announced he was pregnant i.e. writing a play. I had no excuse. I heard myself say 'I'll do what I can.'

I was working on a little gem, *Il Campiello*, a Venetian comedy, which qualified since it was a comedy and was 'short'. I had worked on the translation and it was ready. My head in the lion's mouth. I had seen Georgio Strehler's great production at his Piccolo theatre in Milan. 'Piccolo' is the word. Strehler's theatre was small, like the Cottesloe would be but wasn't yet. The challenge of putting a Piccolo play in the vast Olivier space before Royalty was one, in hindsight, that I should have never considered. I was young and foolish and had never had a flop so 'fail better'. Which we did with all hands.

Campiello was an extraordinarily happy rehearsal period. But as they say in the movies: 'Happy shoot – lousy picture'.

The evening started badly with worse to come. In the foyer, the Queen arrived, looking fabulous. In my director's box the audience arrived looking like mourners at a funeral of someone they didn't really like and who had left them out of their will.

The national anthem in the new arrangement by Birtwistle's choice was strangely strange and oddly normal. The arranger/conductor waved his baton like a signalman in semaphore to a foreign ship that had no understanding of the flags. Somewhere, in there, was the tune. The trumpets were in mutiny against his orders. Her Majesty, I'm sure, was mightily relieved when the cacophony blared to a conclusion.

The American ambassador suddenly hearing the tune, was seen to whisper, silently

'My country 'tis of thee, Sweet land of liberty, Of thee I sing.'

Music over, the ambassador smiled and nodded to the Queen as if the music had been her choice, the way he would have done at the premiere of *The Rite of Spring*. Not the best start to proceedings.

My assistant, Sebastian Graham-Jones came into the director's box confirming 'It's hostile. Pretty hostile.'

Then Larry came on. Now I had seen Laurence Olivier play 'modest' at meetings about *John Gabriel Borkman* when Ralph Richardson decided maybe he would not be available for the Ibsen. He even acted 'blushing' as I suggested to the meeting that he could play the part. Like his Oscar acceptance speech – wonderful, colourful, marvellously spoken. He could read his gas bill and still have a standing ovation.

He started in supplication and ended in heroic modesty wishing his theatre good fortune in the future. We were doomed. No one had ever said less more eloquently.

Standing ovation. Cheers all round. Some tears…

Even the great Beryl Reid and Peggy Mount in our little Venetian comedy won't get a laugh after that.

From the director's box I heard a famous dramatist say to his wife 'I hope this is as bad as I hope it's going to be.'

The first rule of showbusiness – never blame the audience, but it was hard not to break it that night. There is a true story of Alfred Lunt and Lynn Fontanne – giants of Broadway – performing in *The Guardsman* of Molnar.

'I say "Please may I have a cup of coffee?" and there should be a laugh,' said Alfred.

Lynn replied 'Alfred, if you asked for a cup of coffee instead of asking for a laugh you *might* get one'.

That night my gallant troupe didn't ask for laughs – they begged for them. The ill-wishers were unmoved.

We had a less than 'swell' party. The Queen graciously greeted everyone concerned and home we all went.

A flop hurts – deep. Not so much as a man losing his job. Or a miner losing his family and his whole industry. But hurt it does. I was proud of much of the show, especially the first score Michael Nyman did for theatre or film, but there are very few happy memories.

It is hard to finish this piece of the story. Bowed down by the event I went to Sebastian's family bolt hole in Sittingbourne, Kent. I walked. I looked at cows. Autumn turned to winter. I only went back to the National for meetings. The first visit on that overcrowded train I felt, as the *FT* brushed into *The Telegraph*, as the standing City folk bumped together as they stood all the way, that they were still reading my 'mixed' reviews.

Resolved, and with new ideas building, the second journey was much more positive. What the hell – they're reading somebody else's notices or something more important like what's happening in the world – in politics, the economy, the markets, or even the arts. I'm not travelling with them to the City to deal with the problems of the world. I'm on my way to work on something that, hopefully this time, will bring delight and joy to those who witness it.

As Tennessee Williams signs off his notebooks I finish this chapter that bought back some less than happy times.

En Avant.

Mass

by Leonard Bernstein

Leonard Bernstein, 1986

Celebration is my favourite collective noun, as in 'a celebration of larks'. If you have seen the larks ascending in my home in Scotland or in a friend's field in Suffolk, I'm sure you will concur with that magic. So what do you call a group of great conductors – and I mean *great*. I have settled on a 'maestri'.

They were Bernard Haitink, Simon Rattle and Leonard Bernstein. I was to direct *Parsifal* at Covent Garden with Haitink, *The Cunning Little Vixen* of Janáček in Rattle's Royal Opera House debut, and Bernstein's *Mass* as a part of the Barbican Festival devoted to his work and that of his contemporaries. Haitink and Rattle were modest enough. I remember them sitting next to me in the dress circle listening to an orchestral rehearsal of Carlos Kleiber conducting Verdi's *Othello*. Scores in hand, they nodded as they agreed on Kleiber's unique markings and noted them in their scores. Bernstein would never be in such an audience. He, I believe, thought that his own markings were definitive and most would argue that particularly in Mahler, they were.

When it was announced that I was to collaborate with the maestro, my agent in New York, Sam Cohn, had lunch with Lenny's manager, Harry Kraut at the late lamented but never forgotten Russian Tea Room just around the corner from Carnegie Hall.

Harry began 'Well, Sam, it's either a marriage made in heaven or –'

Sam replied ' – the other thing'.

Thank God it was the former. Working with Bernstein was the opening of a door to my interest in classical music. I had not deserted The Beatles, Stones, James Taylor et al but here was Shangri La with a high Lhama guide.

'I'm so glad you're doing this,' whispered the composer after his usual good morning kiss. Over a hundred Guildhall students on tiptoe waited for his benediction.

You could say, however, that *Mass* is a mess. It is a collage of brilliant fragments flawed by attempts at pseudo religion and soppy lyrics.

In a previous production the director thought to 'unify' the work so Bernstein gave him a few days to make his 'improvements'. Bernstein finally heard the unified version and said 'Marvellous. It's much more of a piece'. Once the director had congratulated himself on saving the day the composer added 'So I want all that stuff back in now – I *like* it flawed.'

Nevertheless the 'Reflections' for solo cello, for example, are heartbreaking. As we got to the 'heartbreak' in rehearsal I spoke: 'At this point – nothing happens on stage – we all just listen to the music.' Out of the darkness from the smoke-filled wings, Lenny appeared, tearful or mock tearful we never knew. 'I've spent my life in musical theatre waiting for somebody – anybody to say that!' A pip and a half on anybody's uniform.

The next day could be a Dreyfus case – and so it was. Hayden Griffin did a wonderful design for *Mass*, lit brilliantly by Andy Phillips. One of the unique features was that the conductor's podium was in the middle of the room with an encircled orchestra. Neither Bernstein nor Justin Brown (the assistant conductor) had a problem with this but John Mauceri, the director of the Bernstein Fest did. Now, Lenny had been highly critical of Justin: 'You have no idea 'bout the third ear, have you? None.'

Lenny took over and, in a downbeat, the orchestra improved. The 'Agnes Dei' was alive, at last. Finally, young Brown had to ask the maestro about this third ear.

'Well. The first ear is what you've just heard from the players. The second is what you are hearing, and the third?' after a pause. 'The third ear is preparing the orchestra for what you *want* to hear'.

Justin passed the test.

'That's it! That's the tempo. See what I mean!'

Those of us, all of us, in the absence of Lenny's charisma nodded our heads in affirmative confusion.

After a run-through, conducted haltingly by Mauceri, the following conversation occurred, over whisky in the Bernstein suite at The Savoy Hotel. The cast: the composer, his manager Harry Kraut, and the confidant/director who, like the composer, hates confrontation.

LB: It's obvious. Fucking obvious.

HK: I couldn't agree more.

LB: The kid's [Justin Brown] gotta do the opening instead. Everything else is fine. Just fine.

HK: Apart from the music.

LB: You got it Harry. What a mishigas.

HK: Billy we can't have this fucked.

BB: No, it's good work.

LB: Exactly Billy so Mauceri cannot do the opening. So you better tell him. First thing and tell the kid he's on.

BB: Well, I think ['Why me?' is what I really think] – what about tonight?

LB: We're watching television tonight. It'll wait 'till morning and then you tell 'em – tell 'em both.

So, dreading the next day I waited for the television to be turned on. There was always a piano in the room which Lenny played to us all, always brilliantly after notes (I recommend the scarcely possible piano part in his First Symphony).

The broadcast begins. 'Ladies and Gentlemen' – the commentator dominates the room as the 'pianist' takes his stool in front of the set.

'Live from the Church of St John the Divine in New York City *Requiem* by Andrew Lloyd Webber conducted by Lorin Maazel.

The music started and, almost at once, Lenny was at the keys, quoting the derivatives of *The Requiem* and its influences.

LB: Mahler. Obviously. More Mahler. Is this Ravel? No. No. Fauré. A foray into Fauré. Bitch! No. Not Gustav again.

This reminded me of Florence De Jong accompanying silent movies at the old Academy Cinema.

Somebody from our captivated audience of a show: 'If it's so second hand why is Maazel conducting it?'

'Money,' the pianist replied.

'Would I have advertised a Rolex watch?'

Harry Kraut replied 'The Rolex people didn't ask you.'

Lenny smiled and then hushed us all as he concentrated on Mahler, Fauré, Poulenc and most everybody else.

Mass was a triumph for every student and for Guildhall which gave Lenny a much deserved fellowship. Time passed – too long a time before I was due to meet with Bernstein again.

I did not know how seriously Lenny had been ill. Cordially invited to the Dakota to introduce him to Angela my wife, I picked up the *New York Times* and was astonished by its front page headline. 'Bernstein Dead.' It had to be him. There was only one of that stripe. If anyone contests the greatness of his legacy they should listen his *Candide* overture or to the late

recording of the Tchaikovsky 'Pathétique' or any fugue or riff from *West Side Story*.

I have walked with greatness and called him friend.

At the meeting of teachers and scholars Lenny said 'Trouble is, Billy, everybody knows their own business — plus music.'

Leonard Bernstein

Leonard Bernstein, Justin Brown & Bill Bryden, 1986

Michael Gough & Beryl Reid in 'Counting the Ways' National Theatre, 1976

Edward Albee in rehearsal, 1976

Beryl Reid in rehearsal, 1976
Opposite: Michael Gough in rehearsal, 1976

'Golden Boy' by Clifford Odets
National Theatre, 1984

Boxing

I love boxing. Not as a pugilist, you understand, but as the audience at the main event, preferably at ringside. My companion at the big fights was normally Russell Willett, an Australian psychologist who was then the husband of Helen Montagu, keeper of such purse as we had in Bill Gaskill's heady time at the Royal Court.

Russell liked to do things in style. Drinks at a posh hotel, limo to the venue – maybe even a bet on the outcome. We once had a darts game against Australia by phone link with many a dollar or pound on each throw of the arrows.

The fight was between Smokin' Joe Frazier and Joe Bugner at Earls Court. Russell and I were sipping our champagne in the bar at Claridge's when Frazier's entourage entered. I remember pink silk suits, big brimmed hats of a similar hue, and both of us being referred to as 'Hey dude!' Russell poured the quartet a glass and asked if they were hungry after the long flight from the States. 'Man, we are starved an' parched. 'An thanks for the bubbles – where's the fine restaurant this highly recommended establishment brags 'bout?'

Russell indicated the door to the dining room and the four Frazier fans in their shimmering pink and purple fedoras entered. One of them, Leroy, went over to talk to the diminutive Spanish maître d' guarding the entrance to the empty room.

'Sir you are not allowed in without a tie.'
'How's at?' questioned Leroy, our new friend in pink.
'To enter the dining room you must wear a tie.'
'You can't wear a tie with this stuff, man.'
Leroy, proving his point, entered and was served.
Frazier won.

Another fightnight, Russ and I at ringside. A world championship between John H. Stracey and the little-known Panamanian – Carlos Palomino. At ringside you're just behind the reporters like our best, Hugh McIllvaney, and our worst. There is often a sprinkling of international journalists among their number. There was a guy from New York or Chicago we noticed and listened to. His look was out of Damon Runyon and his voice from a thirties movie. When Palomino triumphed, the voice from the old movie, chewing his old cigar, was heard, quite clearly to say to whoever was listening at ringside: 'Carlos Palomino – Carlos Palomino! He isn't even a household name in his own house!'

from an occasional diary

During a New York trip, sponsored by Paramount I enjoyed a visit to the executive screening room – all Spanish brown leather – and saw an Australian film *Gallipoli* featuring the emerging star, Mel Gibson. Paramount was just about to distribute it as an acquisition. Following the screening the Head of Distribution, Frank Mancuso brought to the table details of the publicity campaign, including the poster. The Great Mancuso was master of image and sales. Remember his tremendous poster of the pram on the mountain with 'Pray for Rosemary's Baby'? This poster read:

'From a place you may never have heard of – a story you'll never forget – Gallipoli'

In the beat that followed Frank waited for his usual 'Mancuso you've done it again.'

I heard my voice say '*I've* heard of it.'

'And you can go fuck yourself!' said the Great Mancuso.

Another *Gallipoli* tale: The music for the film was the wonderful 'Adagio' by Tomaso Albinoni, who died in 1751, long before international copyright, even before the United States of America. Nevertheless the Australian producers rang the superagent, Sam Cohn at ICM.

'Who is the agent of Tomaso Albinoni?'

'I am.' said Sam.

from an occasional diary

There was a gathering, at the White House in Washington, of the giants of the Arts and Academe. Many a donor or sponsor was in attendance. A lot of these benefactors are women and at such a white tie affair many decide not to wear their spectacles. Confusion followed, since everyone had to sport little labels saying who they were, not easy to read with weak sight. One lady sponsor found herself talking to Irving Berlin, the great songwriter but believed she was talking to Isaiah Berlin, Senior Philosophy Professor at Harvard:

'Tell me, Mr Berlin. What do you think is your greatest contribution to twentieth-century thought?'

Irving Berlin replied: '*God Bless America* I guess.'

Tony Richardson
to Bill Gaskill.

'The trouble with you Bill, is that you have no
idea about the politics of show business or
the mechanics of success!'

I think in that generation only Tony himself knew.
In mine I think Trevor Nunn 'fell into it'
because of the surprising success of English
and French musicals.
The present generation of directors seem to
have taken Tony's credo from the breast.

American Buffalo

by David Mamet
National Theatre, Cottesloe

Jack Shepherd as Teach, 1978
Opposite: David Mamet, 1983

It was Biff. Biff Liff was the legendary stage manager on Broadway. His credits included the original *My Fair Lady* (more later) and, to this day he is flown out of town at the producers' expense if a big show is in trouble on the road. At this time, Biff had retired from the prompt corner to become a theatrical agent at the William Morris office in New York. He was my agent in America and my friend.

In the days before email and the rest he sent me a cable – or was it a fax? I have never forgotten the gist, even if I don't remember the detail.

'HAVE JUST SEEN A WONDERFUL PLAY PERFECT FOR YOUR GUYS AT THE NATIONAL. STOP. 'AMERICAN BUFFALO' BY DAVID MAMET. STOP. YOU KNOW HIM BUT THIS IS MATURE. STOP. PULITZER ALL OVER IT. STOP. COPY ON WAY. STOP. AND HE IS A CLIENT. BEST BIFF.'

Me to Biff:

'MAGNIFICENT. STOP. WHAT UNIQUE DIALOGUE – SWEAR WORDS NOT A PROBLEM THIS SIDE OF THE POND. STOP. WE GOT RID OF THE LORD CHAMBERLAIN AT LAST. STOP. COMING OVER TO MEET MAMET SOONEST. EVER. B.B.'

As predicted, the play was wonderful and ideal for the Cottesloe. We had a fine cast for *Buffalo*, a marvellous set by Grant Hicks, who had been doing excellent work at the Traverse Theatre in Edinburgh but now seems lost from the theatre to television and film. There was a problem with Dave King playing Donny, the man who ran the junk shop where the play takes place. I had seen Dave being superb in David Hare's play *Teeth 'n Smiles* at the Royal Court. Dave had been 'big', as he called it, both here and in America as a comedian and recording artist. He was, at one time, the star of his own show on U.S. television when Bing Crosby was on hiatus. When 'big head', as he was nicknamed, met Mamet, egos collided. There was a conflict on a line or two that Dave wanted changed – for no reason in my view. It was 'I know funny' from Mamet against 'Funny is money' from King. Mamet won but left the building. His agent saw the finished show and told the author his play was in safe hands. Peter Hall agreed. In his diaries he described the work as 'seamless'.

Dave King as Donny Dubrow, 1978
Opposite: Jack Shepherd & Dave King

84 | Bill Bryden & David Mamet
in rehearsal for 'Glengarry Glen Ross' September, 1983

Glengarry Glen Ross

by David Mamet

National Theatre, Cottesloe and West End

After *Buffalo* I was determined to keep in touch with Mamet and longed to direct his next play. To prolong our relationship, we considered doing his *Edmond*.

'The fabulous is never anything but the commonplace touched by genius'.

Boris Pasternak

But a new play arrived at Harold Pinter's address. He sent it to both myself and Peter Hall. Pinter had been David's hero and had been told that there had been an unsatisfactory table top reading. Mamet wanted notes. 'Notes,' said Harold 'Eleven out of ten!'

When I read *Glengarry Glen Ross* in manuscript, I *knew* this was a masterpiece. The only other time I had this reaction to a modern play was *Saved* by Edward Bond.

Reader, we bought it and scheduled it for the Cottesloe. Little did we imagine that Olivier awards and even the Pulitzer prize for Drama were to follow.

Harold Pinter was a great help in rehearsal and a continuous lover of the play, which concerns salesmen trying to find buyers for useless land in Florida. I think David thought in rehearsal they were good in parts but not desperate enough. When I asked him to give notes to the company Mamet said 'I have one note – these guys could sell you cancer!'

Mamet stayed with us through previews and triumph. He was particularly encouraging to Jack Shepherd as Roma and to Derek Newark, giving his best ever performance as Shelly Levine.

I remember Michael Linnet, who helped transfer the play to the West End, having seen the film when it appeared much later, saying to me: 'Who would have thought, Derek Newark was a better actor than Jack Lemmon?'

He had a point. While the star-cast film was very good, for me it never had the sense of our group of actors.

The Cottesloe became a centre for the giants of the American theatre. Dustin Hoffman wanted to join the company. Maybe there is still time to work with that wonderful actor. Since then, with Mamet, I have directed his early play *A Life in the Theatre* with Samuel West and that extra special exquisite artist, Denholm Elliott. I am so keen to work with David again.

I've asked my colleagues 'Why hasn't Mamet written a new play as good as *Glengarry Glen Ross*?'

Who has?

Cast of 'Glengarry Glen Ross', 1983 from left to right Derek Newark, Jack Shepherd, Tony Haygarth, James Grant, John Tams, Karl Johnson

from an occasional diary

I have a friend, a handsome Glasgow bookmaker. When he was young, he was 'taken up' by his London bosses who knew he was destined for higher things. He was taken South, wined and dined, mixing with celebrity culture. One evening at Harry Saltzman's club The White Elephant on the River, my bookie friend was stuck in a one-sided conversation with a crashing bore. Trying to escape from the punishment my friend asked: 'What's your name?' 'Peter Sellers,' came the reply. 'And what do you do?' 'I'm a comedian,' said Sellers. My bookie asked in genuine enquiry 'Is this your day off?'

Son of Man

by Dennis Potter

RSC, Barbican

No one who witnessed it could have failed to be moved by Melvyn Bragg's final interview of the dying playwright, Dennis Potter (1935-1994).

In the interview Potter talked of his childhood in the Forest of Dean and his early memories of Baptist hymns by the American composers Moody and Sankey. Their 'Stars in my Crown' was quoted by Potter more than once.

> 'Will there be any stars in my crown
> As that evening sun goeth down
> Will I wake with the blest
> In that mansion of rest
> Will there be any stars in my crown.'

John Tams, also influenced by that great interview, used these words throughout *Son of Man*. They were sung by the deeply talented James Ellis, sadly no longer with us.

Joseph Fiennes played the leading role. I have always had a deep feeling of a bond between us when working together.

John Standing was new to the RSC. Born to the Boulevard, the West End was his home base. After a run-through he asked 'Bill, can you tell me why I'm doing this?' However, his Pontius Pilate was fine and distinguished.

Many of my former Cottesloe Company took part, including Robert Oates, who, as a centurion, was put in charge of Joe Fiennes' safety as Jesus on the cross was about to be hoisted up for the crucifixion. Some nights, at this crucial moment of silent tension, the stentorian voice of the RADA gold medal-winning Bob, was heard to say: 'All right Joe?'

Dennis Potter, 1984
Opposite: Bill Bryden, 1995

Bill Bryden & Joseph Fiennes in rehearsal
'Son of Man' by Dennis Potter, RSC, 1995

The Holy City

The film was commissioned by Michael Grade for a specific Easter transmission on BBC1. I set the Gospel story in present-day Glasgow.

The piece was acted, with great integrity, by David Hayman and every other actor in the cast. Inevitably the film caused controversy, especially in Glasgow. Wreaths were left for me at the door of the HQ of the BBC in Scotland.

In Nobby Clark's picture we have closed down Sauchiehall Street for Jesus to ride into the 'holy city' on a donkey. Too literal perhaps but a golden memory to all of us who were there.

P.S. The story goes that if the above were really to happen the BBC would broadcast 'The Second Coming of Christ' live. Only followed by the announcement 'Viewers in Wales will have their own programme.'

The Holy City, Sauchiehall Street, Glasgow, 1985

Susan Fleetwood as Titania in 'A Midsummer Night's Dream'
National Theatre, 1982

95

Six Characters in Search of an Author

Luigi Pirandello
adapted by Michael Hastings

BBC Television

In these 'snapshots' I have concentrated on my work in the theatre and opera. I have mostly avoided the good times I've enjoyed in film, television and radio. It was only when Pat Chalmers invited me to 're-invent' the drama department at BBC Scotland that I turned from an avid watcher to an officer of the great BBC. Bigger than any Hollywood studio, financed by the public and run by talented people who believe in its ethos, this is where you want to be if you believe, as I do, that broadcasting is a public service.

I was given an open brief to establish the drama department in Glasgow as a network player. In this I was encouraged by Michael Grade's enthusiasm for the work we did and by friends such as Alan Yentob and Jonathan Powell. Michael had been a leading agent, a controller of an ITV network and then head of BBC1. This must have been a foreign country to him but he brought to the corporation a much needed flair and, surprising for a Londoner, the belief that there was talent beyond the metropolis. With

Michael Grade a deal was a deal. When I pitched the idea of *Tutti Frutti* to him, his handshake was worth more than the budget, as was his care in the progress of the project.

Pat Chalmers had set up a unique group of talent for me to head in Glasgow. My deputy, Norman McCandlish, is talented, honest to the core and more loyal to me, than, at times, he should have been. Any success we had there would have been impossible without his attention to the work. I was lucky that such fine writers were up for writing with us. We did two fine films of Peter McDougall: *Down Where the Buffalo Go*, starring Harvey Keitel and *Down Among the Big Boys* with Billy Connolly, produced by my fellow Scot, Andy Park. John Byrne wrote *Tutti Frutti*, our first BAFTA success, and Donna Franceschild created *Takin' Over the Asylum*, our second. I think we made a place in which writers could work, actors could thrive and talent would be cherished. I had terrific creative times with Trevor Griffiths, William McIlvanney and others, mostly resulting in a project that got made. However I didn't have much time to be a director. So I seized the chance to be 'on the floor' for Pirandello's *Six Characters*, one of the plays on the 'Performance' strand helmed by Alan Yentob and Simon Curtis. Yentob agreed that the film should be shot in widescreen black and white which made it

'Six Characters in Search of an Author' BBC Studios Glasgow, 1992

shine out from the rest of the series. The set was by Hayden Griffin, and wonderfully lit by photographer Stuart Wyld. I watched it only the other day and was still impressed by the achievement of all of the talent of the BBC in Scotland.

The play starts with 'the characters' interrupting a rehearsal of Pirandello's *The Rules of the Game*. Michael Hastings and I decided they would enter the shooting of a minor English B-Movie by the likes of the Danziger brothers, who made second feature films in the 1950s, shot at Merton Park or other small studios of the time. (If you understand any of the last sentence you're an old movie buff, like me.) The well-chosen cast were old friends and new – John Hurt, Brian Cox, Steven Mackintosh and, in particular, Tara Fitzgerald who looked amazing in John Bright's authentic period costumes.

Six Characters had many admirers. I remember Trevor Nunn saying 'It was like a lost work of Orson Welles.' Compliments by one's peers are rare. They are cherished.

A final tale of my deputy in Glasgow, Norman McCandish. In phone business to the U.S, the Yanks never got his name. Now, there was no one more gentile than Norman. However, much to my amusement and to Michael Grade's delight, our friends named him 'Roman Hamlisch'. Norman took on the mantle and oftentimes 'Roman' made a deal or two with our friends across the sea.

98 John Hurt as The Father, 1992
Opposite: Tara Fitzgerald as Emily, 1992

Tony Harrison, 'The Mysteries', National Theatre, 1985

Brian Glover as God in 'The Nativity', National Theatre, 1985

This bread that I do bless and break
It is my corse no common crust.
This beakr's t'blood shed for thy sake
And sup of it ilk man you must.

Tony's work on the whole project was uncanny in its accuracy and love of the original and its responsibility of clarity to an audience in the modern world, every member of which was living in the shadow of his or her own doom. He described himself as 'the man who came to read the metre' but of course he was much more than that. He insisted on the dialect being accurate, on the alliteration of the verse being true. He knew that the original poets who had made the plays wrote them in such a way to draw attention to the story, to hold the audience with the story that they knew, and, more importantly, a story in which they believed.

The process of staging the plays began, as it often does, with a director and designer looking at some images. My images were a certain kind of 'appearance' through a gloom. Tangent to that, I wondered how we could duplicate the pageant wagons, namely the play moving from point to point through the crowd. In the original, the crowd waited as the various plays passed by them. Bill Dudley and I agreed that, somehow or other, we had to find a way where the process would be reversed. The audience would somehow pass by the plays. We refined or altered a public kind of performance which we dubbed Promenade Theatre in order to make the tickets sound more glamorous (it's better to say a 'promenade ticket' than 'you've got to stand').

With the promenade solution begun, La Tour and Rembrandt came into play. We decide that the room had to be transformed into a space of moving light and quiet and originality, where the audience who had spent their day in the office and rushed to the theatre through the traffic and noise could find *peace*. In the costume area, we decided that all the actors should be dressed as modern workmen, members of the equivalent of the original trade guilds. So, Jesus was a house painter, Pontius Pilate was a car park attendant, the soldiers who nailed Christ to the cross

'The Mysteries' The Band & Company, 1985
Opposite: 'Doomsday', 1985

'The Nativity'
Brenda Blethyn as Mary and Dave Hill as Joseph, 1985

were going to be a mixture of the modern workmen and an image of the Breughel soldier. Bill Dudley's first drawings of the room, his first images of scenes from *The Passion* and his subsequent imaginative leaps at how to do Noah's Ark or – spectacularly – Adam and Eve in the Garden astonish me yet.

John Tams did the music. Some whole plays had to be sung. Songs had to be written or folk songs found, which told the stories. Just as we asked Tony Harrison to write *The Last Supper*, so we asked John to write a song which expressed the first sight of the cross proceeding Christ's trial before Pilate; 'Lewk up, Lewk up' was the perfect description of this moment.

Top: John Tams, 1985; Bottom: Karl Johnson as Jesus Christ in 'The Passion', 1985. Opposite: Jack Shepherd, Barrie Rutter, Olu Jacobs & Valerie Whittington in rehearsal for 'The Nativity', 1985

'The Nativity' Karl Johnson as Abel and Robert Oates as Cain
Opposite: 'The Passion' in performance, 1985

The Ship

The Harland and Wolff Shed. Govan, Glasgow.

Lazarus Only Done It Once is the title of Pat Lally's biography. It tells his story of the highs and lows of political triumph and much adversity until he became one of the most successful holders of the title Lord Provost of Glasgow. Without Lally's energy there would be no fine Concert hall in the city and, in 1990, Glasgow would never have been appointed European City of Culture.

'Culture?' Many a Glaswegian had Goering's attitude to the subject. In 1990 international stars were engaged – Luciano Pavarotti and Frank Sinatra were booked. From a city whose reputation was based on a meritorious novel *No Mean City* – a story of razor gangs which took two writers to chronicle the period so badly – the 'culture' in the title seemed an ill fit. If it had been 'European City of Humour' it would have been perfect. Billy Connolly and, before him, Jimmy Logan and Rikki Fulton would have embraced that. And the ticket prices! 'A hundred pounds for Pavarotti? – but I think that includes "full board"' was only one cynical gag.

Pat Lally knew it was a challenge but he was in it to win. 'There's lots of stars but there's no show about the city. Glasgow is the star'. This was at our first meeting after I was asked to take part, before the *The Ship* was commissioned.

Lally had seen *The Mysteries* at the Edinburgh Festival. He wondered if there was a Glasgow cycle of these medieval works. I'm sure there was but the texts are lost in time. So, our conclusion was a new, epic show about the city and its river. Thus *The Ship* was conceived.

My wonderful designer and friend Bill Dudley has never been daunted about any idea – no matter how fanciful. 'We build a ship and then we launch it.' That was the concept, and the audience, with many a shipyard worker, believed it. But I'm ahead of my story.

The Creative team for *The Ship* was similar to that of *The Mysteries*. On this project, John Tams, the maker of music, collaborated with the ace accordionist, Phil Cunningham, who also composed some original pipe tunes. I was no lover of the sound of bagpipes until Phil came into our orbit but, as a result, I now understood why the soul of the Scot is at the mercy of it. The lighting was entrusted to the quiet and determined Mark Henderson. The team committed, Bill made a practical model of the space which we used to raise the finance for the show at

many a fundraiser organised at the City Chambers by the Lord Provost.

Funding came from Patrick Chalmers, the controller of BBC Scotland who guaranteed a substantial sum against future television rights. This is before there was a script to read. Pat's other idea was to put the legendary Brian Wenham on our board to, I'm sure, protect the BBC investment.

The board was chaired by the eminent jurist, Sherriff John Boyle who was always optimistic that the project would happen and be the highlight of Glasgow's City of Culture effort, though of course not all the board were as enthusiastic.

At this point, I have to pay respect and gratitude to Eddie Jackson, our producer. Eddie had run Borderline Theatre in Ayrshire and he was very brave to take on the problems of organizing such a unique project.

Finally, after many disappointments, Bill Dudley found 'the space'. The old Harland and Engine Shed in Govan, eventually known to Glasgow taxi drivers as 'The Ship'. The show had become an address.

So we had a design, most of the money and a potentially wonderful space. And, after accusations of rapidness by many (especially Pat Chalmers at the BBC) I wrote the script, keeping Bill and Tams abreast of its development. (See 'Ship's Log, a diary of this progress, coming next.) This was the first production I had done since meeting my new partner, Angela Douglas. She was a tower of strength and encouragement, hosting many a production meeting with good grace and good food at our London home. Until one night when I came home from one of our frequent Glasgow meetings, to find her ashen-faced: 'So you're alive! I called Bill Dudley's girlfriend. He wasn't home either! She's worried sick!'

An aeroplane had been lost over Lockerbie in Scotland at the same time we were in the air. It could have been ours. The Pan Am flight from Frankfurt had been blown out of the sky. No one knows why. No one ever knows why.

Casting *The Ship* was easy and quick. The actors I mention have since died but, without them, the show would never have been the success it was – Tom Watson, Joseph Brady, James Grant and Jimmy Logan, in particular. Jan Wilson and Juliet Cadzow were the female stalwarts and the young bloods (not so young now) were William McBain and Andrew Byatt.

I had seen Scotland win the rugby Grand Slam at Murrayfield and could never forget, the Scots captain, David Sole, leading out the team at a walking pace after England had run on. I had my opening. The company would walk on as a team to John and Phil's music. Whether it was a folk memory of Murrayfield or not, the house rose every night to this overture.

The Ship was, I hope, everything Provost Lally wished it to be. It certainly was for me.

Towards the end of the run we recorded the show for the BBC. At one of these performances we did a charity show for Save the Children for which Princess Anne is a patron. It was decided that it would be fine if she presided over the launch of the ship at the end of the evening. An assistant was sent to instruct her royal highness how to behave in the scene. Her reply: 'I *have* been to a launch before!'

The Cast & Band of 'The Ship', 1990

The Ship's Log

June 1988. A visit from Bob Palmer and Neil Wallace. They've been appointed to direct Glasgow 1990. (They were the organisers of the Glasgow visit of Peter Brook's *Mahabharata* to the Tramway, a former tram shed in 1988.)

Fans of *The Mysteries*, they want something similar from myself and my colleagues. One thing is certain – these men are not afraid of scale. Some of Brook's theatrical 'bravery' has rubbed off on them sure enough. A new theatre space in the city is enthusiastically discussed. 'An Industrial Cathedral'. But what is the show? Very soon into the meeting I hear myself, inspired by their enthusiasm no doubt, talking about building a ship – a liner at that – and launching it. The members of my family who were part of the great days of the Clyde would be characters. The spine of a production seems to be there at the first meeting.

[Note to Bill Dudley (Designer) : We've been invited by Glasgow 1990 organisers to make a big show for their European City of Culture Festival. The idea could not be simpler. We build a ship – a liner in fact – and at the end of the evening it is launched. I'll explain to you in more detail when we meet.]

November 1988. Greenock. Shipyards. Like the folk song 'I was born in the shadow of a shipyard crane.'

The song goes on to the line 'I heard my mother say, it was tears that made the Clyde.'

We're here where I was born in order for Nobby Clark to photograph the cranes, but the cranes are down. It is in my grandfather, Willie's voice, that I remember their magnificence. He worked here and ever after, not a day would pass that he did not look down from the brae reassured by their stature. A beginning…

Script extract:

They looked down. What they beheld astonished them. The view erased all memory as it brought a chill to their hearts. They had stood here looking down to the yard from the brae every early morning since they ceased to be working men at the shipyard's final closure.

The view of the cranes has always been before them, but now, in the space of an afternoon, an evening, and a long dark night, the cranes had vanished and, by first light, were gone forever.

The cranes were down. There was nothing left now to signify a busy shipyard. No memorial…nothing whatsoever…nothing to obscure the view of the river and the cap of snow on the green hills beyond.

DOUGIE: Mem'ries an' rust. A that's left.

PETER: Aye.

DOUGIE: But cuttin' the cranes doon. Like thiefs in the night. I canna credit it. Christ, ye can see Dum'barton or wherever the hell that is over there.

RAB: It's no before time.

DOUGIE: Eh?

RAB: It's about time we realised we're 'back numbers'. Takin' the cranes doon just puts the end tae the chapter. But ye cannea credit it, can ye?

PETER: We'll get used tae it. We're used tae the rest o' it a' ready. What difference this gonnae make, eh? You can see the river clearer for wan thing.

RAB: What's the point?

DOUGIE: D'ye mean?

RAB: What's the point of living down the river noo? Eh? Buy a rod an' see if they're bitin?

DOUGIE: Could dae worse. At least that wouldnae be in the past. We're relics. I tell ye. We're ghosts. This is just the confirmation o' war…

[Note to Bill Dudley:] Thank you for the magnificent drawings of designs for The Ship. I agree with you it would be wonderful if we could secure the engine shed at Yarrow's or some equally large space.

Our commitment should be to a total involvement of the audience, especially in the work scenes where craftsman are working towards the building of the ship.

If we can secure a large space like this there should be enough space around the 'liner' for the audience to be a real part of its progress. I note that 600 people will sit in the 'theatre' you have designed and 400 people will be able to 'promenade' following and in the midst of the action. I'll show the plans to the people at 1990 and I am sure they will be as excited as I am.

February 1989. Glasgow. The search for the 'industrial cathedral' goes on. Glasgow has changed… It's easier to find a brasserie than an engine shed. We lunch in a converted fire station and dine inside an industrial crane. Soon there will probably be a restaurant called 'Shipyard' – the waiters in 'bunnets' and overalls, rivets round the menu and coffee served in billicans…

After much frustration we come across the Harland and Wolff Shed in Govan. A vast space. Not too atmospheric. Not sentimental. An empty canvas for Dudley to work his magic on. Billy Connolly served his apprenticeship here. That's good enough for me. By the way, there is no acoustic. John Tams must come up soon and bring his expertise to bear.

124

William Dudley, Designer of 'The Ship' & Bill Bryden
in The Shed Govan, 1990

[Note to Bill Dudley.] Thank you for your detailed drawings of 'the launch.' I agree that is appropriate that the audience help the workers to remove the timbers and are thus physically involved in the moment when the ship slides away, leaving the empty theatre — the empty space, the empty shipyard.

Script extract:

RODDY: So we're done.

GEORGE: Looks that way. The order book's like a skunk's diary.

RODDY: We did everything we were asked to. Everything required. Is there nothing left of our all that's wanted any more? We were taught the work…as a way o' things…now that's a thing o' the past. Oh, they'll blame the unions. They'll blame the managers (oh, they'll blame you George!) – and me – but it's just progress. Just people in a hurry tae get tae Malaga – or New York. Just people no' havin' the time tae look at the view. An' this hurry….this ramstam'll be the death o'likes o' us. Oh, there'll be the new work. I hop ta' Christ! Maybe there'll be less heart to it and it'll no' be what we're bred to, an' maybe no' what we promised the weans…it's a changed! Don't get me wrong. I've known change. Big changes. We both huv. But this changes the template. The whole malarkey…

March 9.

Sponsorship meeting of *The Ship*'s company. It seems that we are too late for support from some of our target companies. One of board tries to sum up: 'In my view, the horse has bolted. Now I don't want to be the one who pours cold water over the entire project but' – he then proceeded to do just that. They are a good group, however. They are behind us. All they want is to see the script. Being here reminds me of the terrible trials we had in the seventies trying to establish a Scottish National Theatre. With these men and women on board we might have succeeded.

April 21. London.

To N.F.T. *The Magnificent Ambersons*. Angela has never seen it, the magnificence doubled by her enthusiasm. All directors should be forced to see Welles's wonders at least once a year. The last reel. The 'come-uppance'. The lament for the old Indiana. If only one moment of *The Ship* could be as eloquent of times past.

April 26. Govan.

Press launch. A good turnout, all impressed by Dudley's model. Not many photo opportunities in an empty shed. Photographers take us on a trek to find a crane or a bollard – something – but their desired background is long since gone.

July 1.

Casting begins. Former colleagues from the Cottesloe Company asked to join and scripts are sent to actors I've admired but never worked with. Tams sings me the final anthem down the telephone.

'Fading away like the stars in the morning

Losing their light in the glorious sun

Thus shall we pass from the Earth and its toiling

Only remembered for what we have done

Who'll sing the anthems and Who'll tell the stories

Will the line hold, will it scatter and run?

Shall we at last be united in glory

Only remembered for what we have done

Only remembered

Only remembered

Only remembered for what we have done.'

August 4.

Saturday. Off to Glasgow. Rehearsals for *The Ship* on Monday. We begin.

William Dudley on the set of 'The Ship', 1990

The Big Picnic
The Harland and Wolff Shed.
Govan, Glasgow.

Given the chance to explain *The Big Picnic* and what I set out to achieve I have decided on two things. One: not to explain, and two: pay tribute.

Despite the success of *The Ship* in the 1990 celebration of Glasgow as European City of Culture, it took four years to find another epic idea, and the finance, to be able to return to the shed in Govan. To commemorate an anniversary of the Great War, it was decided to dramatize the story of a Glasgow battalion going to the front.

'It's wonderful here in France… It's just like a big picnic' – Julian Henry Grenfell (1888-1915) Killed in Action.

I had the subject, indeed the title, but in big shows without commercial guarantee, the most difficult job is often raising the money the budget demands. As in all things, truth is the first casualty. Broken promises prevail but there are always surprises on the way – but that's ahead of my story.

Ross Harper, a distinguished lawyer in the city, became chairman of our board, which consisted of the great, the good and the indomitable, among them Janey Buchan, always enthusiastic, her social conscience full of energy and wisdom. Also on board was 'the banker' whom I referred to as Polonius. He was the banker in the game of musical chairs who could not find a seat.

The first member to actually put his hand in his pocket and produce a cheque was Murdoch MacLennan, then Chief Executive of Scotland's most popular newspaper *The Daily Record*. His enthusiasm for the project delivered free advertising, ticket concessions and cash. Murdoch's generosity was followed by welcome support from Pat Chalmers for the BBC and the Lord Provost, Pat Lally, on behalf of the city. Blue skies indeed!

The weather in Glasgow can turn skies to grey and rain on any optimistic fundraisers' parade. The first money is secure, it's the rest of the money that's the problem. This is where one meets, worst of all, 'acting heads'. These are deputies who have criticised the *real* head for years and wished him or her either on permanent leave, or preferably, dead. The one we met I will call 'Dr Dee'. He was a number two at one of the grant-giving bodies and his enthusiasm was seemingly genuine: 'When have I been here before?' I remembered Hollywood and such meetings. 'Who are you seeing at Paramount?' (or any studio) You give the name and those in the know, identify a junior vice president. They tell you 'Good guy' or 'great girl, she'll be head of the studio one day.' But not today.

'The Big Picnic' in rehearsal at The Shed, Govan, Glasgow, 1994

So the result is your 'green-lit' project is stuck on a permanent amber on the road that is development hell. So it was with Dr Dee on *The Big Picnic*.

The first meeting where minutes were taken he assured us 'I love this project. This is exactly what we should be supporting. I can offer you (enormous sum)!' The chief returns and there's a second meeting. Back to being deputy, Dr Dee says 'I deny I ever said such a thing or offered such a sum!' The good news is that he was fired. The bad news: the project did not get a dime from his organisation. Fundraising is not only subject to false arrogance of this kind but prone to potential corruption.

These were, and still are, the days of health and safety. It is impossible to get a licence to admit the public to a new building without several signatures on the certificate. In our case, one of the 'judges' appeared to be reluctant. If this happens you cannot open, no matter how much money you have raised or tickets you have sold.

'I think he's on the take.' Jim Higgins, my builder and friend, whispered to me in a corridor.

'Who?' I replied.

> JH: The guy won't sign
>
> BB: What does he want?
>
> JH: We've got to get a lawyer. A Catholic lawyer. They do buildings.

BB: Why don't we just get a good one?

JH: £500 would pay him off.

BB: Are you sure?

JH: No. I guess that's his price.

BB: This is blackmail.

JH: Absolutely. But you could call the Provost.

I called Pat Lally and told him the sad tale. He said: 'This city was as corrupt as Chicago in the olden days.' He paused 'but that's not happening on my watch. Give him the money.'

Where do you find £500 on a Friday night, forty-eight hours before opening? My associate producer Crozier has a brother who owns a very successful pub with, thank goodness, the precious £500 in the till. Jim Higgins did the 'handover'. I rang Provost to tell him that the deed had been done. I inquired what would happen to the greedy culprit. 'He's a memory' came the reply.

So, after many such adventures, our licence was granted and *The Big Picnic* opened to great success. I remember it with fond memories, tinged with great sadness, since it was the last time I worked with my late friends, Morag Hood, Jimmy Logan and Iain McColl for whom the parts were specifically written. All in all, it was a great company event. In the programme I wrote about my colleagues and the spirit of collaboration.

In my professional life, I have never had a closer collaboration than with Bill Dudley, John Tams, Phil Cunningham, Stuart Hopps and Sebastian Graham-Jones. The parts of this show that are theirs are sometimes hard to measure. You see in the programme the specific work that is their responsibility, but it goes beyond that. Sometimes a song is suggested by a designer and sometimes a plan of design by a maker of tunes. This is genuine collaboration and the work of a fine creative family. I thank them.

'The Big Picnic' Company, 1994

'The Big Picnic' in rehearsal, 1994

Sir Ralph Richardson won a Lifetime Achievement Award given by the Evening Standard.
He said he was proud, but dismissed pride as a mortal sin. Having released himself from guilt, Ralph
concluded — 'So — I shall paddle in a puddle of pride for the rest of the day.'

Sir Ralph Richardson, 1981

Remembering Ralph

Anyone who was ever touched by the magic of our own Prospero figure, that unique actor, Ralph Richardson, has a tale to tell.

He had wonderful, but occasionally crazy ideas like indoor fireworks – this resulted, almost, just almost, in the burning to the ground of Notley Abbey, the country house of Laurence Olivier and Vivien Leigh.

Peter Hall has the tale of a hair-raising journey on the pillion of Ralph's motorbike at high speed, only to be told, at journey's end and to his distress that Ralph did not want to do Falstaff (his greatest role) ever again.

I never worked with him on a part but he showed great encouragement when he saw my productions. He also wrote me letters. One I remember had the letterhead 'Ritz Hotel, Paris'. It began, 'Here I am in the old pub.'

I remember a television broadcast at the premiere of David Lean's film of *Dr Zhivago*. All the actors, one by one, came up to the interviewer to supplicate on the experience of working with Lean in Madrid.

Deification was the order of the day. 'Marvellous,' said one. 'A unique experience,' said another. 'To be aware of such talent and wisdom,' said a third who was, indeed, Rod Steiger. When it came to Ralph: 'A bit of a holiday really.'

Ralph, after the show or when 'resting', served a unique cocktail. I doubt if it's on the list at Harry's Bar in Venice or the American Bar at the Savoy Hotel in London. The drink consisted of a large Gordon's Gin *and* a large Stolly Vodka with a twist of lemon and ice, if you insisted.

Christopher Morahan, my colleague at the National, was invited to Ralph's lovely house in Regent's Park (where his great collection of vintage clocks were wound by Ralph, personally, every day) to see if he would agree to appear in Christopher's next production. I think Ralph had agreed after the second cocktail (the recipe I outlined). The next morning, I was with Peter Hall in his office when I happened to ask how Morahan's meeting had gone. Peter decided to phone Ralph. His reply: 'Chris Morgan – Chris Morgan – nice fellow – can't hold his liquor!'

Duncan Weldon, the producer with whom I have had great success and luck in the West End and whose enthusiasm and care I have appreciated over many years, tells a tale of lunch at The Ivy (when it was the H.Q. of showbiz, run by Jeremy King and Chris Corbin) with Ralph and John Gielgud. I think Duncan was trying to get them to revive *Home* by David Storey.

Lunch over and the Bisquit begun, Sir John excused himself since he was booked to do a voiceover or a commercial. After the Bisquit Weldon invited Ralph back to his office for yet another drink. Now, Duncan's co-producer, Paul Elliott is responsible for the most important pantomimes, up and down the nation. That year one of the shows was *Snow White and the Seven Dwarfs*. When Ralph and Duncan came into the outer office there were, at least, twenty-seven dwarfs waiting for their audition. Ralph passed them without comment.

After more drinks and a deal done, they both went through to the outer office. Ralph, who thought he might be victim to a hallucination earlier, turned to Duncan and said, exquisitely astonished: 'They've gone!'

Billy. There are two kinds of director. The first, well he's like the captain of the ship. 'We're bound for South America. On the voyage we'll dock at Madeira, Rio de Janeiro, even Maracaibo, until we reach Buenos Aires!'

The second kind asks 'Where would you like to go?'

Ralph Richardson

from an occasional diary

Peter Daubeny, long remembered for organizing the Aldwych World Theatre Seasons, decided it was Ireland's turn to be one of the countries involved. It was obvious that the Abbey Theatre was the company to invite. On offer was a less than brilliant production of *Juno and the Paycock* by Sean O'Casey. Daubeny went to Dublin to see a run-through and thought it just about passed muster. But the set? Not up to World Theatre standards in Daubeny's opinion. After much discussion with the designer on how the set could be improved, the Dublin voice of a stage hand could

be heard from the wings. 'What the fuck does an Englishman know about Georgian architecture?'

On the first night of the same production of *Juno* all the famous Irish actors working in London were in attendance to applaud their own national theatre – Peter O'Toole, Niall Tóibín, T.P. McKenna, Norman Rodway, Siobhán McKenna, J.G. Devlin et al.

Looking at the programme and disappointed with the players billed, Devlin turned to O'Toole and declared: 'Christ, Peter – there's a better cast in the audience!'

Peter O'Toole as Macbeth, Old Vic Theatre, 1980

Peter Hall

I am not the only director who would have been less successful without the constant encouragement of Peter Hall.

Brave, political, fair, with an extraordinary appetite for work, a great director of plays and opera and a unique impresario, he is the only one who had the grit and determination to open, despite all the struggles, the new National Theatre on London's South Bank.

Whilst writing this minor memoir of Peter I was asked by a newspaper in Scotland to review the Australian director Michael Blakemore's new book *Stage Blood*. I said no.

I cannot vouch for that part of Blakemore's book which is about working with Laurence Olivier. But what he has written concerning his ill relationship with Peter Hall and a number of his associates, I seriously question almost all of it. I was there.

It is not for me to go into chapter and verse of this book. A dark mood of envy and spite prevails. I was reminded of the director John Dexter's view of Blakemore. 'Bill, it is a well-known fact that there is no love lost between myself and the wily Aussie.' But enough of that.

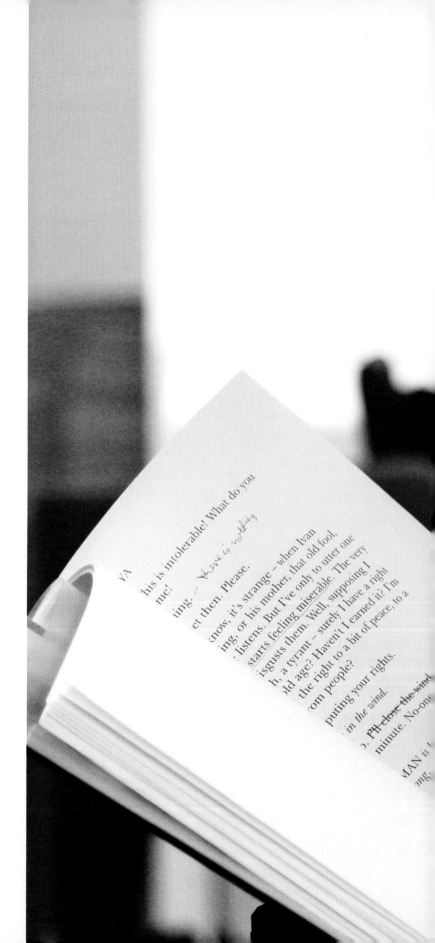

| Peter Hall in rehearsal, 2007

140 | Peter Hall in rehearsal for 'The Oresteia', National Theatre, 1981

Later, the opportunity of being invited by Peter Hall to run the Cottesloe Theatre was a demanding and exciting one – giving me the scope to develop the dream I had long nurtured: a popular theatre both with music and dance. I could now begin to build my dream team, all talented and innovative – all 100% committed.

I invited Keith to join me in the adventure. Christopher Hill's landmark history of the English Civil War *The World Turned Upside Down* was an early success for the company. But *Lark Rise* was unique, and like *The Mysteries*, a promenade production.

We started the work by visiting the Oxfordshire hamlet of Juniper Hill (the real 'Larkshire'). Bill Dudley studied its flat land and lowering sky and devised a magical design in which the sky was dominant, the light passing through from dawn to dusk. Rehearsals were most pleasurable once we slowed the tempo to reflect the peace and quiet of the country. In performance I remember that a highlight was when, bringing scythes to the 'field', the actors appeared to scythe the audience as if they were corn.

My next project with Keith was his version of *Don Quixote* in the Olivier. With Paul Scofield as the Don and Tony Haygarth as Sancho, how could it go wrong? But it did. Keith's version was not up to his usual high standard or the production up to mine.

Keith and I still share much, including our undiminished support of Manchester United. But after *Don Quixote* Keith went south (to Australia). I went north (to BBC Scotland) and our relationship went west.

Old Movies

This was my one and only attempt to write a commercial play. Perhaps I was bored of being labelled 'promising *Scottish* writer' or just that I was at an age when anything appears possible.

I put into the work everything I knew about Hollywood but, as William Goldman rightly says on that subject, 'nobody knows anything!'

I have heard every excuse for a play or production not working including the show coinciding with the Chelsea Flower Show. I can think of no excuse as to why *Old Movies* didn't quite come off.

It was a great pleasure to work with my old friend, Fulton Mackay and my new one, that fine American actor E.G. Marshall (*Twelve Angry Men – The Chase*). I expected the notices to be somewhere between my usual ones, which normally ranged from 'flawed masterpiece' to 'some telling scenes'. And my usual they were. The good news was I had a congratulatory card from John Osborne which I will always treasure. Of course, at that time John's favourite commercial play was *Pyjama Tops*.

Opposite: Peggy Ashcroft
in her dressing room at the National Theatre, 1980

from an occasional diary

I'm with the wonderful Scots actor, John Laurie. Nowadays, he's most famous for being in *Dad's Army*. But as a young actor he played Hamlet at the Old Vic and was most terrifying as Peggy Ashcroft's jealous husband in Hitchcock's film of *The Thirty-Nine Steps*. I went to his cottage to talk about verse in preparation for a production (sadly unrealised – yet) of *The Tempest* at the National Theatre. Talk turned to gossip of two giants of the stage:

JL: 'Bill, are you still at the National Theatre?'

BB: 'Yes, John.'

JL: 'Well, John Gielgud – his besetting sin is the voice beautiful. The voice beautiful, John Gielgud. And Laurence Olivier. His besetting sin is self-regard. Laurence Olivier. Besetting sin. Self-regard laddie.'

BB: 'John, what's your besetting sin?'

JL: 'Malice, laddie, malice!'

149

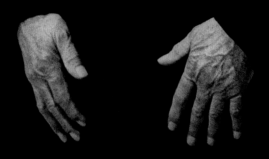

Laurence Olivier

In preparation for this book I looked again at some of the photographs Nobby Clark has taken during his recording of the British theatre of his time.

One picture struck me, in particular. It is of Laurence Olivier on his birthday. It is a portrait of a great man, getting older but still full of strength and, especially, charm and charisma. I was fortunate to be invited, many times, to Olivier's country home in Sussex, in his last years.

He would be frail of a morning and then, just before lunch, his legendary energy would return and, for more than an hour he would be on top form.

On one occasion, he turned to me and said 'I do not remember the first time that we met but I will not forget the first thing I said to you.'

I knew it was in the huts in Aquinas Street, then the HQ of the National Theatre at the Old Vic. I was there waiting for Bill Gaskill, and about to become his assistant at the Royal Court. That's as far as I could remember apart from a vague recollection that, at the time, Olivier was pondering that some of the younger actors in the company – Anthony Hopkins, Michael Gambon and others – felt they had graduated from their apprenticeship and ought to be given bigger roles, even leading parts.

It is hard to describe the unique sound of his voice, but I can always hear it clearly in my head, saying: 'I do not remember the first time that we met but I will not forget the first thing I said to you.' (Then, a pause, worthy of Pinter) 'Billybaby – What the <u>fuck</u> are we going to do about Derek Jack-obie!'

A triumph and disaster was the great Olivier saying the line 'No more of that.' at the end of *Othello*. Due to the understandable customs of our time, only black actors are now chosen to play the role. The Moor of Venice is a great step in any classical actor's journey from Hamlet to Lear. All actors should be allowed to play it.

Sir Laurence Olivier on his 70TH birthday, 1977; Opposite: Sir Laurence Olivier on the stage of the Olivier Theatre for the opening of the National Theatre, 1976

152 Derek Jacobi & Trevor Eve in rehearsal for 'Uncle Vanya' by Anton Chekhov at Chichester Festival Theatre, 1996
Opposite: Frances Barber as Sonya & Derek Jacobi as Uncle Vanya in 'Uncle Vanya' at Chichester Festival Theatre, 1996

Peter McDougall

'I carry a brick on my shoulder in order that people may know what my house was like.'
Bertolt Brecht

'That pipes the morning up before the lark
With shrieking steam, and from a hundred stalks
Lacquers the sooty sky; where hammers clang
On iron hulls, and cranes in harbours creak,
Rattle and swing, whole cargoes on their necks;
Where men sweat gold that others hoard or spend,
And lurk like vermin in their narrow streets:
This old grey town
Is world enough for me.'

From 'Greenock' by John Davidson

Writing for the screen is hardly Britain's greatest contribution to world cinema. There are exceptions – Graham Greene (of course), Harold Pinter (his collaborations with director Joseph Losey), Bryan Forbes (*The League of Gentlemen*) and a few others. Sometimes the folly of the commission and the casting of the screenwriter turn the project awry. Whose bright notion was it for instance, to have Tom Stoppard, eminent though he is, to bring *Billy Bathgate*, E.L. Doctorow's novel about Dutch Schultz to the screen when the director of the movie, Robert Benton had already written *Bonnie and Clyde* in a similar genre?

In movies for television, Britain has been much more fortunate. The times bring forth the men and women. Such a time was when the BBC embarked on 'Play for Today' and mined the talent that abounded in that fertile period. The commissioners included producers Tony Garnett, Innes Lloyd, Graeme MacDonald, Kenith Trodd and Ann Scott who first encouraged, in my view, the cream of the crop, Peter McDougall.

Peter came, as I did, from a working family in Greenock. It is said that the changing geography of the town can only be seen by watching the historical progress of his films. A sad tale – from busy shipyard to a Tesco where the slipway used to stand.

Just Another Saturday (Prix Italia) was his first success, to be followed by many others. My personal favourite is *Just a Boy's Game* (directed by his favourite director, the late John McKenzie, produced by Richard Eyre and starring the singer Frankie Miller in his first acting role).

When I was at BBC Scotland I developed two of Peter's films. *Down Where the Buffalo Go* with Harvey Keitel and *Down Among the Big Boys* with Billy Connolly. Working with Peter can be abrasive and challenging for a producer but the work is always in the pursuit of excellence.

I always hoped that my protégé, Tessa Ross, would succeed me as Drama Head in Scotland but she has gone on to higher things, heading Film 4 and the National Theatre. Tessa would have coaxed another masterwork from Peter McDougall. None of my successors or their kind has done so. It would seem they are searching for the next franchise, not the original voice.

Classic tapes of Peter's work are available, I'm sure, in colleges offering media studies degrees under a tutor who may never have burned in the crucible of showbiz.

The present situation in the BBC has nothing of the enthusiasm of the past. This is not nostalgia but a sense of loss of the encouragement of talent – of love of the work.

Peter McDougall, 2002

Does Samuel Beckett's work need to be cryptic and incomprehensibl[e]
of All That Fall in Dublin, **Peter Lennon** found that it suddenly ma[...]

Falling for Beckett

Cinderella at the National Theatre: (left to right): Robert Stephens as Euphoria, Derek Newark (Gloria) and Susan Fleetwood as Prince Charming ...

British panto back in fashion

By David Hewson

Two years ago the traditional British pantomime was pronounced dead. Now the painted dames, sackcloth horses, and leggy principal boys are sufficiently back in fashion to give their customary reply — "oh no, it isn't".

Four pantomimes, if you count *Peter Pan*, are being presented in the West End of London during the holiday, more than any Christmas for a decade.

Last year, nearly a quarter of a million theatregoers flocked to the West End after Christmas. Bookings for the period are running so high that most of the shows are expected to sell out in the next few days.

The flourishing pantomime business is reflected in the provinces where the Christmas show is frequently the one profitable highpoint in the theatrical year.

Advance bookings for the pantomime at the Theatre Royal, in the East End of London, had reached 25,000 by the end of July, and stood at 38,000 by the beginning of this month. Local firms, schools and unions have bought whole houses. Mr Mark Borkowski, the theatre's spokesman, said this week: "Frankly, I am having trouble fitting the press in.

One of Britain's leading pantomime impresarios, Mr Paul Elliott, is promoting 13 shows from London to Belfast, and two abroad, in Canada and Zimbabwe.

The National Theatre has entered the pantomime business for the first time this year with Cinderella. Its director, Mr Bill Bryden, said that the production, which opens on December 15, will have its quota of ugly sisters and standard pantomime jokes.

"We have been trying to do a panto for years but have only just got around to it. I just think it is a good opportunity to get back to some of the kind of values and performances that aren't associated with television or modern influences, to try to tell a fairy story. It is innocent, simple entertainment."

The National has searched Edwardian and Victorian archives to come up with authentic scripts and the pantomime will not contain topical jokes, unlike many of its rivals and the popular Royal Shakespeare Company adult pantomime-cum-musical *Poppy* at the Adelphi.

Whether the box office promises of the rash of new shows will be kept through January is something which will continue to give impresarios sleepless nights. But for the moment, they are happy to welcome the successful pantomime back into the theatrical fold.

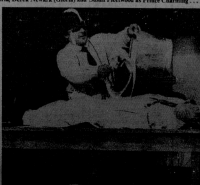

... The 'slosh scene': Anthony Trent and Stephen Petch[...]

ARTS

How they built the Somme in a shed

A vast engine shed on the Clyde is the venue for a £1 million theatrical experience, opening next week, about a battalion of Glasgow soldiers in the First World War. **Robert Gore-Langton** went to see it take shape

THE disused Harland and Wolff engine shed in Govan is a monster of a building. You could almost fly a kite in it. Here the company used to produce engines and parts for liners, including, it is said, the Titanic. Until recently it was just another grimy part of Clydeside's abandoned industrial landscape. The building, however, is now enjoying a new lease of life. Like other vast European structures that have been invaded by the performing arts (for example, the former Fiat complex in Turin and the old Zeppelin factory in Hamburg) the Glasgow shed has become a temporary theatre.

You won't find any gilt, plush or swag curtains, mind you. The Shed offers unfrilly drama with rivets on. For the past few weeks, it has again become a noisy hardhat area. Local workmen have been building a stage meant to resemble the battlefields of Flanders 75 years ago. The raised stage is 57ft wide, 250ft long and covered in earth. Thousands of turves have been laid green side down, the brown stage then dotted with shell craters, pools of mud and trenches.

On one side the audience will sit in a special mobile 'grandstand' and will be towed up and down beside the stage, following the soldiers as they retreat and advance amid theatrical mustard gas. At times, the audience will even be able to wander out onto no man's land. A band — with pipers — will be playing overhead, suspended on a mighty bridge crane that travels the length of the roof. The whole thing is costing £1 million.

The show, written and directed by Bill Bryden, is called *The Big Picture*. The play tells the story of the recruits of the Highland Light Infantry's special City of Glasgow Battalion — their enthusiasm to serve and the subsequent reality of the front. The only thing ironic about it is the title, taken from one soldier's ecstatic description of the war in a letter home. The play is not at all sneery or bothered with blaming the generals. It is more of a tragic episode, with plenty of period Rab C. Nesbitt patter, about the pals who left Sauchiehall St for the Somme.

The cast playing the battalion have been issued with period 303 rifles, a heavy machine-gun, spades, pickaxes and khaki uniforms. A former drill sergeant has

been hired to lick this shower of mincing Scots thespians into shape with kindly advice and a few choice threats — "Get it right or I'll tear your arms off and hit you with the wet ends!"

Bryden the playwright can't seem to leave Glasgow's working-class history alone. In 1972 he wrote *Willie Rough*, a play about his docker grandfather. In 1990, he wrote *The Ship*, which was the first play to be done in the Shed. His father had been a shipfitter, and the play was an affectionate look at Glasgow's doomed workforce of platers, welders and riveters. During each performance a ship was actually 'built' and launched down a ramp. Now the same creative trio — Bryden again writing and directing, with designs by Bill Dudley and music by John Tams — are presenting a similar pageant-like play about Glasgow at war.

"The idea was to tell the Great War story through a volunteer force from Govan," says 52-year-old Bryden. 'How the different

professions muddled together as they went through Moss to the Somme. I had one grandfather who had been in Ypres who never talked about the war. The untold secrets of warfare, the private reactions, the articulation of the inarticulate, if you like, struck me as really worth examining.

Dreadful though they were, the First War and the bombings of the Second caused less destruction to the Govan community, Bryden reckons, than the decades of recession and unemployment that have followed since.

"The injury to local pride, the vanished dignity in the labour and craftsmanship for which the Clyde was famous for centuries, was a more crippling blow than either the Blitz or the coffins coming back from the Somme to Glasgow Central station."

The design concept — a theatre 'installation' in effect — will be part of the evening's experience. When Bill Dudley researched the show, he was "struck by the fact

that armies on the front were within shouting distance of each other. They often weren't much further apart than the length of our shed. The military advantages were so small — they were measured in yards — they could actually be represented.

"The other thing I thought was that the First World War gave this century its abiding image — the wasteland. I once visited the trenches in Ypres and I've pushed hard to get across a sense of that landscape.

"The Shed is also an environment that makes you aware of the Machine Age. It's a very apt place for our play about mechanised war and mass destruction."

Much of the action will be stylised. There will be no blood and guts. One supernatural feature is also included in the play — the well-documented phenomenon of the Angel of Mons. This was a vision or mass hallucination which appeared to thousands of men in the trenches. In the play the angel will be portrayed by Deborah Pope, an "aerial artist", ethereally clad and balletically twisting from a wire 50 feet over the stage, appearing at the play's emotional highpoints.

In the Erskine Hospital for veterans, outside Glasgow, there are six soldiers who served in the Great War. I visited one of them — the delightful Jimmy Cook, 98 this month, the hospital's best darts player. He survived both Passchendaele and Ypres.

He never personally saw the Angel of Mons. "But I believe those that did see it. I believed them absolutely then and I still do," he told me, tears welling in his eyes at the thought of his dead comrades. You realise, meeting the likes of Mr Cook, the risk this sort of show runs of becoming a glib or impertinent memorial.

But Bryden is clearly regarded by the locals as "one of us", and he is both passionate and sincere about his city, its people. Sassenach viewers may occasionally wish for subtitles.

"The indomitable human spirit of the Glasgow people marches on today," says Bryden. "I hope that their humour and their optimistic streak is there in this play. It's not all about carnage and Armageddon."

The Big Picture runs from Sept 14 to October 30. Tickets. 041-242 3[...]

'Rehearsal of a scene in which the 'Angel of Mons', played by an aerial artist, appears to the troops

Bryden (left), Dudley and actor Jimmy Logan

156

ARTS

[M]ysteries were a big hit for the National Theatre 20 years ago. Now they're ba[ck]
[...]heir distinctive style work in a changed world, asks leading actor **Jack She**[pherd]

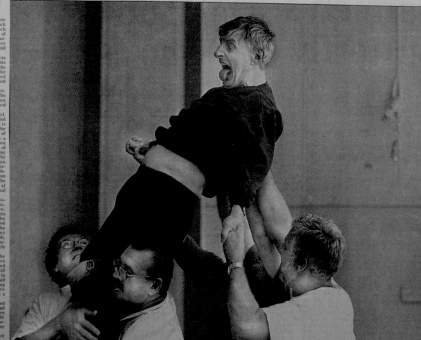

[...]pherd (aloft), who played Lucifer and Judas in the first production and does so again in the new one, with members of the cast of *The M*[ysteries]

The spirit of the age

THERE are ghosts in the rehearsal room. Brian Glover is no longer with us, nor

[sep]arate plays telling the Bible story from Genesis to Revelation. Each play was funded by a separate Guild and acted

[...]tions, God and Jesus had "spoke posh" — it was only the lower characters that spoke in dialect[...]

It was a very rare thing in British theatre history — a genuine company, and it

It's a bit sad now to come back and see that there's little evidence in the building of

It's the clo[...]
to finding o[...]
popular the[...]

Samuel Beckett, 1982

Watch it Come Down

by John Osborne

National Theatre, Old Vic and Lyttelton

John the brave. John the beginning. The man who, in 1956 at the Royal Court, opened the door to the modern British theatre. Without John Osborne there might have been no Christopher Hampton, no David Hare and no Edward Bond. Certainly someone like me would never have thought there was a good life in the theatre.

This play *Watch it Come Down*, which I directed, was I suppose caviar to the general but it contained several telling scenes and many a passionate speech.

The instinctive and intelligent actor, Frank Finlay, had a scene in a restaurant with his sulky teenage daughter. Love between them had been long lost. The scene was probably based on Osborne's relationship with his only child, Nolan. Frank played the seemingly personal words superbly. It had flaws but the cataclysmic ending of the play when the yobs blew up the converted railway station was the first sign in the theatre that forecast the terrorism to come to us all.

Osborne used to receive abusive letters signed 'Angry. Hendon.' He was sure 'Angry' was a woman. He even picked her out in the front stalls on the first night. As the curtain fell to a mixture of cheers and boos – 'Angry' energetically shouting her disapproval. Frank turned to Susan Fleetwood and whispered 'What's she saying?' While they continued to bow, Sue translated, using her cut-glass accent: '*Money beck. Money beck.*'

John's then wife, the actress Jill Bennett, a magnetic personality anyway, was superb in the play. I thought also she was wonderful for John. She was the epitome of 'chic', her exquisite figure, head to toe in Chanel. She would have been the first to wear the red soles of Christian Louboutin, if they had been available at the time. Jill was also quite a 'wit'. She matched John blow for blow. They reminded me of Mirabell and Millamant in Congreve's *The Way of the World*. Maybe the barbs of wit hurt as much, caused as much pain, as the flying ashtrays. It saddened me deeply that they had such an angry parting.

After the play John asked me if I would like a gift. I suggested a signed copy of *Look Back in Anger*. Taking a crate of champagne ('Bolly' being his favourite) from the boot of his vintage Alvis, John